The American History Series

SERIES EDITORS

John Hope Franklin, *Duke University*

Abraham S. Eisenstadt, *Brooklyn College*

Arthur S. Link
Princeton University
GENERAL EDITOR FOR HISTORY

Paul K. Conkin
VANDERBILT UNIVERSITY

The New Deal

SECOND EDITION

HARLAN DAVIDSON, INC.
ARLINGTON HEIGHTS, ILLINOIS 60004

Library of Congress Cataloging-in-Publication Data

Conkin, Paul Keith.
    The New Deal.

    (The American history series)
    Reprint. Originally published: New York : Crowell, 1975.
    "A note on New Deal historiography": p. 103–108.
    Includes index.
    1. New Deal, 1933–1939.   2. United States—Politics and government—1933–1945.   3. Roosevelt, Franklin D. (Franklin Delano), 1882–1945.   4. United States—Social policy.   I. Title.   II. Series: American history series (Arlington Heights, Ill.)
[E806.C6   1987]   973.917   87-8896
ISBN 0-88295-722-8

Cover design: Roger Eggers. Cover illustration: Clifford Berryman. Library of Congress.

Manufactured in the United States of America
91 90   13 14 15 TS

EDITORS' FOREWORD

Every generation writes its own history, for the reason that it sees the past in the foreshortened perspective of its own experience. This has certainly been true of the writing of American history. The practical aim of our historiography is to offer us a more certain sense of where we are going by helping us understand the road we took in getting where we are. If the substance and nature of our historical writing is changing, it is precisely because our own generation is redefining its direction, much as the generations that preceded us redefined theirs. We are seeking a newer direction, because we are facing new problems, changing our values and premises, and shaping new institutions to meet new needs. Thus, the vitality of the present inspires the vitality of our writing about our past. Today's scholars are hard at work reconsidering every major field of our history: its politics, diplomacy, economy, society, mores, values, sexuality, and status, ethnic, and race relations. No less significantly, our scholars are using newer modes of investigation to probe the ever-expanding domain of the American past.

Our aim, in this American History Series, is to offer the reader a survey of what scholars are saying about the central themes and issues of American history. To present these themes and issues, we have invited scholars who have made notable contributions to the respective fields in which they are writing. Each volume offers the reader a sufficient factual and narrative account for perceiving the larger dimensions of its particular subject. Addressing their respective themes, our authors have undertaken, moreover, to present the conclusions derived by the principal writers on these themes. Beyond that, the authors present their own conclusions about those aspects of their respective subjects that have been matters of difference and controversy. In effect, they have written not only about where the subject stands in today's historiography but also about where they stand on their subject. Each volume closes with an extensive critical essay on the writings of the major authorities on its particular theme.

The books in this series are designed for use in both basic and advanced courses in American history. Such a series has a particular utility in times such as these, when the traditional format of our American history courses is being altered to accommodate a greater diversity of texts and reading materials. The series offers a number of distinct advantages. It extends and deepens the dimensions of course work in American history. In proceeding beyond the confines of the traditional textbook, it makes clear that the study of our past is, more than the student might otherwise infer, at once complex, sophisticated, and profound. It presents American history as a subject of continuing vitality and fresh investigation. The work of experts in their respective fields, it opens up to the student the rich findings of historical inquiry. It invites the student to join, in major fields of research, the many groups of scholars who are pondering anew the central themes and problems of our past. It challenges the student to participate actively in exploring American history and to collaborate in the creative and rigorous adventure of seeking out its wider reaches.

John Hope Franklin

Abraham S. Eisenstadt

PREFACE TO THE
SECOND EDITION

I first wrote these four essays on the New Deal in the summer of 1965, or a full decade ago. It is hard for me to grasp the changes that have occurred in America in that one decade, impossible to gauge the exact changes that have occurred in my own beliefs and preferences. Memory is very deceptive. I cannot, with any confidence, describe my exact state of mind in that distant and hot Maryland summer. When I try, I find too many later intrusions subtly shaping and coloring and often dignifying the self-portrait. I can only cite the external context with assurance, and I doubt that it had much to do with the content of the book. In 1965 the Johnson administration seemed to pass the point of no return in Vietnam. Escalation had led to full-scale war. I attended the first national teach-in in May of 1965, and there heard a historian closely identified with the New Deal defend Kennedy's and Johnson's Vietnam policies. By then a student and faculty antiwar movement functioned on most campuses. But, unless my memory deceives, I was not yet aware of the breadth and diversity of the developing discontent.

Despite my use of several evaluative perspectives, and my inclusion of some predominantly analytical sections, my first goal in writing the book was very traditional: to provide students with a succinct account of the major domestic policies adopted during the Roosevelt administration. Ironically, these largely descriptive sections did not weather as well as the analysis. Almost every new monograph on the New Deal revealed some inaccuracy or distortion. Since most of these errors involve only a few words, or a few sentences, and since my former account remains closer to conventional understanding, these mistakes have become much more of an embarrassment to me than to most readers. But my desire to correct them, to adhere to what I now believe to be the truth, led to this revision. Additionally, in the years since 1965 I have become much more concerned with precision in language. At many points I had resorted to conventional but still exceedingly ambiguous labels (such as "capitalism"), all of which I have tried to amend in this revision, not in order to communicate any different meaning but in order to communicate more exactly.

Perhaps not surprisingly, the evaluative sections of the book received the most comment and were most often anthologized. They have also led to varied speculation about my own views or intentions. The very diversity of labels affixed to the book, or to me, shows that I was not very self-revealing or, perversely, that I must have provided several false clues as to my identity. Noting this does not mean that I am now preparing a soul-baring confession. To make clear my own philosophy, my own deepest commitments, would take another book. To assume an eager audience for such a disclosure would be to flirt with arrogance.

I am sure about one rather obvious motive in 1965, and one I frequently remarked to students. I wanted to demythologize the New Deal, and thus clear the way for a fuller and fairer understanding. I drew upon a growing body of reliable scholarship, which alone made possible such a book. But pervading even the most scholarly revelations was a monotonous, often almost reflexive, and in my estimation a very smug or superficial valuative perspective—approval, even glowing approval, of most enduring New Deal policies, or at least of the underlying goals that a sympathetic observer could always find behind policies and programs. This implied, also, an acceptance or commendation of much that was America in 1965, and particularly those aspects most shaped by New Deal changes. In this sense, most New Deal historians, even if not intentionally, had been self-revealing, for they all seemed to reflect a near consensus of political and economic preferences. Since their work was so value laden, yet so uncritical and consensual, I believed it exercised a subtle and unintended moral tyranny over the developing values of impressionable students. In effect, most New Deal histories were standing invitations to vote Democratic, to value federal initiative, to accept and applaud strong presidential leadership, to accept a welfare state and an indirect fiscal and monetary management of the economy. Most historians seemed to offer precautionary warnings against fundamental dissent, and thus tended to anesthetize any criticism except that increasingly irrelevant and safe variety that they so carefully directed at unfairly caricatured and mythical old Republicans.

In 1965 I know that I did not intend to reverse the near unanimity of New Deal cheers by a single and unqualified series of deprecatory judgments, although some readers still find that intent somewhere between the lines. In this revision I carefully examined each paragraph, and found as many characterizations of New Deal programs that, by my values, seem as praiseworthy as damning. I surely reflected no disenchantment with the New Deal; I had never been enchanted. Besides, any scorecard of value judgments has a parochial aspect. Obviously, the very same characterization of Roosevelt ("he was in no sense an intellectual") will seem a form of praise to some readers, an indictment to others. But to an extent that I cannot now gauge, I am confident my own preferences did influence my choice of language.

In any case, a decade later a rich diversity of dissenting views abounds, and fundamental valuative conflicts have even invaded our formerly genteel historical profession. In such a world the perspectives I offered now approach the commonplace, the ignoble fate that time so often decrees for any history. Now, with most moral dragon slayers positioned in their several well-armed and clearly labeled fortresses, historians may well push their moral conflicts outside the pages of their histories and preach their sermons from other pulpits. In their recognized diversity, they may join in the common task of understanding the historical New Deal in all its complexities—its sources, goals, and enduring consequences. They now realize that, for each consequence, the enthusiastic cheers will mingle with equally fervent and, in our uncivil era, often obscene expressions of condemnation. Thus, very shortly, the most evaluative or self-revealing sections of this book, which I have tried to nourish toward greater clarity but in no case revise or remove, will appear as a historical document, a source for trying to unravel some of the strange foibles of young historians in the mid-sixties.

Fortunately, I usually did not intrude my own views but presented the valuative perspectives of forceful critics of the New Deal, and particularly those of Tugwell and Hoover, neither of whose views I fully embraced then or now. I did find their quite divergent perspectives both coherent and persuasive, and thus good tools for sorting out the very lack of coherence and valuative consensus in the complex programs of a New Deal that had continuity and a common identity only because of the opaque personality of Roosevelt. Such an ideological frame of reference, either borrowed from an articulate but eventually frustrated New Dealer, or from the most eloquent spokesman of a defeated party, or from even more extraneous and uninvolved philosophies (American pragmatism, Southern Agrarianism, Marxism) seems indispensable if we are to reach the fullest, multidimensional understanding of what the New Deal actually meant, what changes it engineered, and thus what we are as a people often directly conditioned or shaped by these changes. In this sense, multiple and often very critical perspectives not only help students reach a more sophisticated personal judgment about what was good and bad in the New Deal (a nonhistorical purpose), but helps them more fully to understand the past. They can view the New Deal in the light of multiple other possibilities that might have been realized had their forefathers been very different people, and thus in a position to make very different choices. These options were not, in one sense, live options for our progenitors, but they are, if understood, options in our present, and it is such options that give poignancy to the past. This is only to reiterate the conclusion of the book, or the one section in which I very carefully chose every word. The rightful focus of any seeming criticism of the past is our present.

I said all this with some fervor in 1965, because the only real anger I had was for so many people in that present, including historians, who seemed unable or unwilling to consider a wide array of moral options. In the enthusiasm of youth I may have been unfair toward my elders, toward those who seemed so satisfied with our national achievements. This anger surely accounts for the judgments that end chapter 3, judgments that I shared with older New Dealers whom I had known. I could understand a glowing celebration of near full employment in the foreshortened perspective of massive unemployment in the thirties. But I had enough lingering agrarian sentiments, enough loyalty to the idea of economic freedom, to believe that, on a higher plane and in broader perspective, the most critical problem for America was not unemployment but employment, with its dependent and servile attributes. I could see praise for a welfare state if the only perspective was the insecurity of the early thirties, but I have never been able to affirm governmental paternalism as more than an interim accommodation, as an ultimately poor substitute for universal participation, for the sense of socially beneficial contribution, for some opportunity to share in ownership and management.

But this line of argument only explains a very small section of the book, and may come close to a presently acceptable apology for things I wrote with much less clarity of purpose in 1965. I easily fall into a reverse snobbery, and offer all my sympathies to losers and underdogs. I respond to the sentiment of Nietzsche—a person of noble character always defers to those below and snubs those above him. I still believe we should be very suspicious of all political winners. They are dangerous because they are powerful, and what wisdom they possess behind the always beguiling and often blinding appeals that insured their victory always has ample opportunity to flower in all its brilliance. Meantime, we should most assiduously search out all possible wisdom in those who lose. They pose no threat, and their valuable and ever so fragile insights may all too soon perish with their lost cause.

CONTENTS

ONE

Roosevelt

The New Deal was an exceedingly personal enterprise. Its disparate programs were unified only by the personality of Franklin D. Roosevelt. Every characterization, every evaluation of the governmental innovations from 1933 to 1938 terminates and often flounders in this personality. Characterization is ever hazardous: least so of men who construct a coherent, articulate system of beliefs; most so of men who, like Roosevelt, operate within conventional, unarticulated beliefs and, in addition, retain a disarming simplicity. Even in the best of circumstances, biography reflects the catalyzing influence of the biographer and thus usually reveals the often fascinating chemical compound of two interacting personalities.

Today only a small minority of Americans remember Franklin Roosevelt, at least with more than vague images of childhood. Unswayed by his vital presence, ever less impressed by his recorded speeches, unmoved by his increasingly dated political concerns, young Americans are baffled by the continued passion of their parents or grandparents, by the subdued fervor of professors, by all oldsters who still dare confess their love or who ever yet vent their hate. They note the touch of reverence in the books of Arthur M. Schlesinger, Jr., the adulation of an aged or departed court—Rosenman, Tully, Tugwell, Perkins, Morgenthau. They also note the last echoes of bitterness from right-wing critics, who continue to identify an almost unbearably conventional Roosevelt with both domestic and foreign treason. Surely the sympathetic portraits are more revealing. Hate is a poor vehicle for communicating personality. But even the best portraits, conceived in love, often seem unlovely to another generation.

Roosevelt, as president, gave millions of Americans a transfusion of courage. They still remember. From his confidence, his optimism, they gleaned bits of hope in times of trouble and confusion. This was Roosevelt's only unalloyed success as president. It was a pervasive aspect of his administration, yet tied to no policies and no programs. It was the magic of a man, based as much on illusion as on reality. There was much to fear in 1933, as there is today. Only fools or gods believed otherwise.

Roosevelt's unusual and politically invaluable self-assurance was the legacy of an unconventional childhood. The bounds were set by a rigid, possessive, but loving mother (Sara Delano); an elderly, increasingly ill, indulgent father (James Roosevelt); a large farm estate, with trees and gardens; nurses, tutors, and loneliness for other children; a patterned, almost regimented tempo of life; and such Victorian virtues as duty, honesty, and fair play. An only child of this marriage, breast-fed, with no competitors for a mother's love, catered to by innumerable servants and relatives, indulged by gifts and toys and pets, young Franklin was secure and happy, reflecting a vitality and commanding presence often observed in single children. The world was his opportunity; he had nothing to fear, so much to master. The focus of his secure world was the carefully managed estate at Hyde Park, with its planted and tended forests, sleek herds of cattle, and carefully cultivated fields. Less serious but more important to a boy, he could hunt, fish, ride to hounds, watch birds, and, joy of joys, sail on his beloved Hudson. Along with stamp collecting, birds and boats were to be lifelong hobbies. Conservation of natural resources, a near-romantic love of trees, concern with agricultural problems remained deep commitments always colored by happy memories.

Roosevelt's boyhood security depended on wealth, but wealth securely fitted into traditional family values. Even in the late nineteenth century, few families could afford an ample mansion, tutors, servants, books and music, and yearly trips to European bathing places. In both the Roosevelt and Delano families, financial security was a product of several generations of effort, mostly in commercial and navigational enterprises and, in the more distant past, in early Hudson Valley land grants. James Roosevelt, at least in his later years, appeared to be an English country gentleman, supervising his estate and serving mankind through local Democratic politics and as vestryman in the Episcopal Church. This was the life he loved. But he was also a financier, with several speculative ventures in his past and always enough conservative investments to safeguard his chosen way of life. He served on corporate boards, invested heavily in coal and railroads, and had participated in business deals looking toward monopoly. The competitive, challenging, acquisitive, often brutal world of corporate enterprise provided a sharp contrast to gentleman farming, even as New York City sharply contrasted with Hyde Park. But to James Roosevelt, and to his young son, the important world was always Hyde Park. He subordinated all else to it. His avocation was really his vocation. Business, a game that he had to play, lacked any but instrumental purposes. Adequate wealth was a social necessity, not an appropriate goal.

Young Franklin loved competition. He loved to win. He wanted to be in the center of things, in command if at all possible. Games gave an outlet to his love of power and mastery. Yet his boyhood required no vital competition for wealth, parental approval, social standing, even grades. His person was invulnerable. He played all games to win, no holds barred. But he never had to fight for dignity, for a livelihood, for a constant input of love to compensate for a horrible lack of self-respect.

For this reason, he never quite understood a driving, acquisitive outlook. He always saw the world as a country squire. He disliked cities unless they could be planned to look like country estates. He always trusted farmers and believed with Jefferson in the generative impulses of soil and woodland. In the 1920s he was boldly speculative in a series of financial endeavors but never displayed the grasping, predacious impulse of so many less secure investors or corporate directors.

Throughout his life Roosevelt would be disarmingly casual about personal finances and about the common necessities of life. He played the stock market as he played ball—to win. He wanted others to play the economic game as he did, and never quite understood those who, driven by need or personal insecurity or controlled by the habits of the marketplace, sought economic power as an end, struggled for advantage with deadly seriousness, tried to gain and maintain privileges of all sorts, and above all did not live up to a gentleman's code. In disbelief, in shocked indignation, in misunderstanding, Roosevelt later denounced such people as economic royalists, traitors to their class, betrayers of their position in the community, and sinful trustees of their inheritance. But at times of deepest political involvement, he played the political game with all the seriousness, and all the cunning, of the most fervent business tycoon and characteristically identified his political ambitions with the interest of all the people.

A commanding self-assurance also insulated Roosevelt from intimate involvements with people. Yet few men were ever more attuned to people and less attuned to ideas. Few men ever possessed a greater art of breaking down barriers in others. The very lack of intimacy, of a compelling emotional need to possess or love another, contributed to his ease in developing a friendly comradeship with multitudes of people. He loved the adoration and attention of people, even to the violation of all his privacy. With consummate art, he played for his audiences and won their plaudits. Some grew to love him and projected onto him their hopes and joys and deepest longings. They invested so much in the relationship; he invested so little and invested so broadly.

This unequal relationship prevailed even in his own family. While a law student at Columbia University, he married Eleanor Roosevelt, his distant cousin and a niece of Theodore Roosevelt. In so many ways his opposite, she fascinated him, and to an extent always did. He idealized and admired her; probably to the limits of his ability he loved her during the first years of marriage. But not as she loved him. Reserved, shy, lacking self-confidence, sure that she was unattractive, extremely sensitive to the feelings of others, she yet radiated a beauty of character and a charming seriousness in outlook. Her childhood had been very unhappy. Cursed with an alcoholic father, an unintentionally cruel mother, orphaned by ten, reared by a stern grandmother, immersed in an exciting but neurotic household, she only slowly gained any sense of self-worth. Much of this she gained from friendships, or by charitable efforts in New York City. The attention of a gay, handsome, confident Franklin was a great flattery and promised a haven of security. Eleanor never forgot.

Yet to a great extent she was shut out of her husband's life. Self-centered and seemingly insensitive, he remained largely unaware of most of her tribulations. Sara Roosevelt not only tried to dominate Franklin (he evaded her efforts) but for years did dominate her daughter-in-law. As five children came in rapid order, Eleanor, easily more perceptive and sensitive than Franklin, had to wait years before she could gain a clear sense of personal identity. Then, after disillusionment and suffering because of his neglect and his now well-publicized infidelity, she moved confidently into the world on her own. Even in their early married life, Franklin never showed any compelling need for intimacy, and never shared his most important thoughts. The children adored and enjoyed their father but suffered from his lack of involvement. For discipline or understanding they had to turn to their mother. At critical family junctures, he might be out playing poker with cronies or enjoying a fishing and sailing holiday. Franklin was like a gay uncle who periodically entertained the children by play or some adventure. They loved him all the more, for they identified him only with pleasure. In the same sense as he accepted his wife and children, Roosevelt accepted others into an enlarged family circle. He was never exclusive. Louis Howe, his political manager, and Marguerite (Missy) LeHand, his secretary or, by his own son's later but much challenged account, even his lover, gave him complete devotion and loyalty to the point of adulation. Just as with Eleanor, he accepted them, used them, flattered them, but never reciprocated in kind. As a self-assured, godlike person, he allowed all devoted disciples to bask in his charm, draw strength from his surety, and eventually share in his fame. Maybe he needed them to shore up some jealously hidden fears. But to have revealed the need would have broken the bond. They flocked to him because of their own insecurity and need and his supreme strength.

Most biographers have speculated about the effect on Roosevelt of his 1921 bout with poliomyelitis, its crippling aftereffect, and his years of unsuccessful efforts to restore his legs to more normal use. Roosevelt was protected from the worst facts until recovery was under way. Eleanor may well have suffered as much mental anguish as he. By the time he accepted the worst, if he ever did, his buoyant optimism took over and nourished false hopes of nearly complete recovery. With all his competitive zeal, he tried to win this game, too, and came closer than weaker men could have. He never lacked this type of courage. His failure to find a cure had no evident, long-term effect on his personality. He seemed the same person in 1928 as he had been in 1921. In many ways his legs became a major political asset, appealing to all who suffered, who had calamities, and who aspired to overcome them. Polio made an aristocratic Roosevelt into an underdog. For him it replaced the log cabin. It also brought him to Warm Springs and helped to create his sincere and flattering interest in the South and to insure him a strong southern following.

Insulated from fear, Roosevelt was also free of doubt. Intellectually, as socially, he exuded confidence. As long as he eloquently asserted, in very broad outlines, the more conventional and traditional beliefs of Americans, he could inspire this same confidence in others and strengthen them by his sense of certainty. But searching inquiry is a product of doubt. Roosevelt never doubted important beliefs. At times he seemed unable to perceive crucial issues or to make careful distinctions. His curiosity was unlimited, but also undisciplined. His keenness in judging and directing subordinates did not carry over to judgments between abstract concepts. He had no inclination to press forward into the subtleties and perplexities of philosophic reflection. His interest in most subjects reached a saturation point when he grasped the broader results of the more general themes. This prepared him for his forte—the active and fighting side of life.

This characteristic bent for action, so typical of many politicians, makes it very difficult to probe Roosevelt's most basic commitments. But it in no sense precludes such commitments. All people have beliefs. That is, they all have predispositions to act in certain ways given the opportunity. By abstraction, these predispositions can be formulated as beliefs or doctrines. But active men, such as Roosevelt, seldom try carefully to articulate them or to make them consistent or to criticize them even when glaringly inconsistent or contrary to accepted knowledge. Other people (the very opposite of Roosevelt) become so entangled in conceptualization, in the problems of consistency and correctness, that they impart intellectual indecision into their actions and suffer terrible anxiety with every difficult choice. Roosevelt did talk about certain commitments, such as to "democracy," but in such vague and general terms as to be almost meaningless except as a type of verbal assurance. But however vague, however inarticulate he may have been in expressing them, his most basic beliefs remained firm and constant.

Roosevelt's unswerving commitments developed in his childhood at Hyde Park, solidified in his years at Groton and Harvard, and never changed during the rest of his life. Groton, an elite preparatory school, gently led him away from his protective family but not into a new intellectual world. Episcopal, English in inspiration, simple to austere in habit, it apotheosized his already acquired virtues of honor, fairness, and service. The headmaster, Endicott Peabody, firm and awesome in direct contrast to a tolerant father, remained for Roosevelt a lifelong symbol of authority, a type of commanding conscience. The Groton curriculum was classical, with manners, taste, and moral habits more esteemed goals than sheer intellectual attainment. The moral tenor was high, the theological sophistication very low. Somewhat out of place in America, Groton was thoroughly Anglican and Tory, shaped for an almost nonexistent aristocracy, honorable, broadly but sincerely Christian, tradition-bound, but very responsible. Roosevelt fitted Groton far better than the sons of most industrialists or the sons of older Bostonian Puritans, whose sharp intellects could never safely absorb the unquestioned verities of Peabody. No student more completely or enthusiastically absorbed the values of Groton— noblesse oblige, manly Christianity, civic duty, and love of God, country, and Groton.

At both Groton and Harvard, Roosevelt displayed a characteristic love for athletics, for physical vigor, and for fraternity. He showed much less respect for academic achievement. This valuation was not a product of youthful irresponsibility, but a lifelong affinity. He certainly, even with his poor to average grades at Harvard, was more gifted as a student than as an athlete. He never made any varsity teams, but he always loved the strenuous life, competition, and comradeship. Team athletics and fraternal organizations gave outlet for his love of power, his desire for leadership, his preference for people over ideas. He did fall in love with books, but usually not to read. These joined his earlier love of stamps and boats as collector's items. He turned his one great achievement at Harvard—editor of the *Crimson*—into support for the football team and an increased school spirit. He gained from Groton and Harvard a veneer of academic sophistication. He learned European languages and achieved some knowledge of ancient classics. He picked up the typically broad and random smattering of information and ideas found in undergraduate courses, and would always be sufficiently agile to learn quickly when need required it. Yet, except for Peabody, no single teacher seemed to make a significant or lasting impression. No courses reoriented his beliefs or, for that matter, even touched them.

Roosevelt lived in the comforting perspective of an undoubted and probably never rigorously defined God and in the easy assurance of the Church. He rarely discussed religion, and apparently never thought deeply about it. But here, surely, rested much of his optimism, his sense of destiny and purpose. His God gave assurance of a meaningful universe in which human effort had cosmic significance. Likewise, he loved the vast panorama of America in the same fervent and unquestioning way that he backed Harvard's teams or cherished the trees at Hyde Park. The problem was how to do God's will, not to define or justify Him, and how to serve America or aid the team, not whether such devotion was justified. His attachment to the land and to a vague "democracy" was equally firm but ill-defined and ill-supported. But simplistic and conventional as they often were, his beliefs limited his actions and focused his lifelong commitments. Exempt from formal inquiry, from serious intellectual probing, he never questioned his deepest affirmations. As persistently as most other American politicians, he refused to carry on a disciplined dialogue between policies and fundamental beliefs. By clever rhetoric, he always equated the two.

Roosevelt's intellectual stance combined the attitudes of a country gentleman and a stereotyped athlete. God, country, college, estate, family, party, team—he revered all these. He gave honor, loyalty, dutiful service to each. He obeyed the established rules and codes so long as they were fair. This often formal, traditional outlook supported Roosevelt's antiquarian interests, his collections and memorabilia, concern with genealogy, alumni support, and competitive partisanship. Here were the unquestioned verities. He labored for them and within them. So, in roughly similar fashion, did most people. When general in conception and when clothed in persuasive rhetoric, his simple commitments proved invaluable political assets. In times of depression, war, despair, cynicism, such elementary loyalty, unburdened by doubt or disturbing questions, communicated an assurance so deplorably absent in events. His faith could preserve a society at a time when courage was more needed than penetrating insight.

Roosevelt's beliefs, though broad and unexamined, were never equivocal. Not only did he refuse to accept new systems of belief, but he rarely understood them fully. When he applauded Christians and democrats, he assumed everyone, at his best, was included. He sincerely commended both Jefferson and Jesus, without trying to understand the complexity of either man. Atheism was beyond his ken. New political ideologies surely reflected evil instead of possible alternatives. He won over opponents by persuasion or dismissed them as traitors. He generously assumed that his beliefs, so ill-defined, so lacking in structure, included almost anyone. He never concerned himself with nuances, with careful definitions. But he was not so generous at the level of power. Here he could be as ruthless and as intolerant as the occasion demanded, since he always too easily felt that he worked in behalf of the vast majority of righteous people.

Above all, Roosevelt was not a pragmatist, at least in any philosophical sense of the word. If the term "pragmatism" has specific meaning, it is a very loose label for a major philosophical movement, which originated in the moral and esthetic thought of Puritanism and Transcendentalism and in the epistemological innovations of Charles S. Peirce, which acquired a psychology and other suggestive, if confused, ideas from William James, and which climaxed in the neo-Hegelian system of John Dewey. For pragmatists, the method of inquiry, although developed in a very complex and technical fashion, was only a prelude to intense moral, religious, and, most important, esthetic concerns and, beyond these, a distinctive and very pious stance toward Being or Nature. Thus defined, pragmatism represented the most comprehensive, and possibly the most difficult, of modern philosophical movements. In his traditional attitudes and beliefs, his lack of philosophical concern, his generalized but simplistic religion, his lack of esthetic sensitivity, Roosevelt was the very antithesis of pragmatic.

Because of its vast scope, pragmatism incorporated some beliefs that almost everyone shared (including Roosevelt), but these took on quite definite and subtle meaning in the context of the whole philosophic outlook, and all rooted in a distinctive metaphysical position called radical empiricism. Nothing indicates that Roosevelt ever studied pragmatism or even came close to understanding it. Few people have, and nothing in his intellectual makeup invited such a strenuous effort. Even the idea of experimentation, as articulated by Dewey and implied in modern science, did not relate to Roosevelt's haphazard, theoretically attenuated programs. His antipathy to theory was close to the anti-intellectualism and common sense of most active men but bore no relationship to the technical interplay of reason and experience in the pragmatic conception of inquiry. In fact, Roosevelt was most unpragmatic in not appreciating the vital instrumental role of formal thought. Only if pragmatism becomes a poor synonym for practicality (a term ambiguous enough for anyone) can Roosevelt, by some miracle of historical inexactitude, become a pragmatist. Even his acclaimed willingness to learn by experience (not distinctive to philosophic pragmatism by any means) has been overemphasized. In very few cases did he ever repudiate any of his past choices or frankly admit the failure of one of his policies. This is not to deny the large number of pragmatists or near pragmatists who were in the New Deal and who helped shape the policies of some agencies. But, as a whole, they envisioned much more sweeping changes and more controlled planning than Roosevelt ever desired or supported. John Dewey, the grand old man of the movement, was always a persistent and penetrating critic of the New Deal.

Lack of intellectual discrimination is not always, in all situations, an unrelieved liability. As an active and busy man, Roosevelt admittedly was not equipped to make any great contribution to American political thought. In no sense was he a Jefferson or even a Woodrow Wilson. But although not an intellectual, Roosevelt was neither an anti-intellectual nor a pseudointellectual. He had no pretensions as a thinker. Thus, unlike some politicians, he never tried to sponsor half-baked ideas or truistic clichés or homilies as if they were the substance of eternal truth and never became a slave to rigid but superficial dogmas. The very lack of structure and subtlety in his beliefs precluded narrow and inflexible policies except when his ego became deeply involved.

Unlike pseudointellectuals, who have the empty form but not the mature substance of a philosophy, Roosevelt moved easily among men of diverse ideas. He never formed a narrow, exclusive political church. Widely varied ideas neither threatened nor disturbed his own invulnerable verities, nor could any of them convert him to a new point of view. He simply did not understand at that level. He liked people and included intellectuals in his circle of friends and advisers. They gave him speeches, bills, needed arguments, and delightful conversation. They also flattered him. Out of their searching insecurity and perplexity, many of them responded to his charm and assurance. He armed them and their valued ideas with power and exalted them into seats of importance. He was their tool for redeeming mankind; they were tools for his enjoyment, for his success in playing the game of politics, and for his own moral attainment.

Even with authentic intellectuals, such as Rexford G. Tugwell, Roosevelt established more of a personal than a philosophical identification. Always looking for new paths of action, hating indecision and inaction above all else, Roosevelt wanted useful ideas. He tried to get a broad grasp of problems and, when interested, could absorb and retain vast quantities of relevant facts. But he preferred to remain at the level of common sense and immediate tasks. He delighted in ridiculing the expert or the theoretician, often with justice. Yet, his inability to probe a bit deeper, to question a few fundamental issues, handicapped him as president. When more critical and coherent prescriptions seemed necessary, he was incapable of supplying them. Yet his own limitations were those of most Americans, and his very conventionality often proved a political asset, even as Woodrow Wilson's broader grasp of abstractions occasionally proved a liability. Roosevelt quickly sensed the political danger even of ideas he personally accepted. But his inability to articulate a coherent body of beliefs, to turn his religion into an honest and limiting creed, to fashion a consistent and operative political and economic philosophy, often left him helpless and confused when confronted with new and unanticipated alternatives.

Broad and general purpose, however fair-minded and generous, cannot substitute for controlling hypotheses. It can, at best, only provide a moral criterion for guiding wasteful trial-and-error expedients. Roosevelt's vague goals restricted the possible and excluded many expedients. He was not an opportunist. His ideas were operative. But he never had the ability to bring unity or rational order to his own actions or to governmental programs. He was constantly forced to whitewash chaotic policies with moral rhetoric or to silence apt criticism by partisan cheers.

Roosevelt's beliefs were not superficial; just his level of discourse and understanding. God, liberal democracy, and even country living can be precisely defined and elaborately justified. But definition is limitation and exclusion. The American political tradition, from John Adams to John Calhoun to John Dewey, had been continuously enriched by an ever more complex and suggestive defense of a constitutional and yet responsive government, but with every refinement the prescriptions became more precise and specific. Instead of the best of many worlds, the honest man must eventually make the best of one world. Too often Roosevelt's disciples or later apologists read into his beliefs some appealing and sophisticated but limiting rationalizations that simply, on the record, were not present in Roosevelt's own thought. Rexford Tugwell tried this, and still believes Roosevelt really understood and accepted his own coherent economic philosophy but, as a habitual politician, never let on. Other biographers, such as Arthur M. Schlesinger, Jr., have attempted the difficult task of turning mere vagueness into a type of profundity. By the same error, critics, blinded by surface maneuvers, partisan rhetoric, or personally distasteful programs, often credited Roosevelt with a vast, coherent, but heretical and conspiratorial philosophy, and in this way make him an even more mythically potent intellectual than the apologists.

Roosevelt, a man of many hobbies, had only one profession—politics. Here his qualifications matched his unparalleled achievements. His success was a function of personality, developed skills, and excellent advice, plus the usual accidents of time and place. Cagey advisers and speech writers usually neutralized his political liabilities—impetuosity, a tendency to overstatement, and egotistic miscalculations. Except for his first, almost freakish election to the New York State Senate in 1910, when only a boyish twenty-eight and just three years out of law school, Roosevelt's political strategy was always in part the work of someone else. In fact, it is impossible to sift Roosevelt's own personal role from that of countless advisers. As most successful politicians, he was soon an institutional person. In 1912 and again in the critical twenties, Louis Howe's careful, meticulous planning of long-range goals and of campaign tactics seemed an ever-present antidote for Roosevelt's irrepressible and often undirected energies. No adviser was more loyal or subservient than the gnomelike, increasingly ill, Howe, Roosevelt's perfect alter ego. By 1928, and his successful bid for governor of New York, Roosevelt acquired more self-restraint and also a much larger political staff, with Samuel Rosenman, Edward J. Flynn, and James Farley rising to dominant positions. But political managers, like jockeys, win only with good horses.

Above all, Roosevelt could persuade. This was his prime political asset. He was never a great orator. In retrospect, his speeches were rarely brilliant and never as eloquent as they seemed at the time of delivery. The best content, even the best phrasing, came from the many speech writers, particularly Raymond Moley. The effect came from Roosevelt's superb delivery. He created a sense of intimacy, of special sympathy and concern, or else a sense of comradeship, of being on a good team, or unified in support of a worthy and mutual cause. Variously a coach with a pep talk, a preacher with simple but pointed moralisms, or a military commander giving encouragement to the weary, he attained a sense of community with even hostile audiences. In small groups, or with one person, he was even more successful, using persuasion to alleviate the sharpest disagreements.

Bereft of deep intimacies, immune to the allure of abstractions, Roosevelt's life was oriented toward people, not as bosom friends but as companions, admirers, or needy recipients of his gifts. His antennae were attuned only to people, to their reactions, their desires, their needs. He sought their appreciation and approval and the sense of power this approval gave him. Always he had a sense for the dramatic and dashing, the arresting gesture or word. The very absence of involvement with his family, the lack of agonizing self-criticism, freed his agile mind for the near infinite minutiae of politics—the flattery of names remembered, the tidbits of personal or local history recalled, the sincere attention to each person's petitions, the superb ability to listen, the facile comprehension of, or near-hypocritical agreement with, almost any idea. His catholic interests, his boyish eagerness and enthusiasm, his love of banter and teasing, his vanity about his hobbies, all endeared him to others. A wonderful master of ceremonies, he entertained well in large or small groups and easily dominated every social occasion. Regrettably, as any good raconteur, he was either a polished and proficient prevaricator or a master at self-deceit, conveniently forgetting or transforming the past. Incidents of his life, and many that never occurred, were more highly colored with each telling, with Roosevelt slowly rising to the very center of every stage.

Politics is a terribly complex pursuit but a rewarding art for those who find satisfaction not alone in the ends furthered but in the game itself. With Roosevelt, the personal, even esthetic rewards were so important that they can never be clearly separated from the moral goals that he sincerely pursued. He even enjoyed enmity if it allowed him the wonderful excitement of battle. At the same time that a Roosevelt policy seemed to serve the interests of the nation, its persuasive appeal was also a tool for his political artistry, and might be used to trick or best a political opponent. Even ill-chosen programs, despite their concrete results, were often political assets and enjoyed accordingly. Roosevelt found creative fulfillment in politics (he might have found it in the military had he been allowed to follow an early interest in a naval career). The voters were the subject matter of his art. He loved to mold and form them into a pattern of his own choosing, yet be willing to choose a pattern in terms of his limited and in part unalterable subjects. As all successful artists, he was able to effect many of his designs, even when they proved poor ones. Persuasion was his brush and his chisel.

Roosevelt, in both his early and later political career, tended to mute issues, unless they clearly contributed to massive popular support. In a little over two years as state senator (the only elected office he held until 1928), he was a rhetorical progressive, but hardly gave content to the ambiguous label except in his fervent support of conservation. Neither then nor later did he display any grasp of the often subtle divisions among those who identified themselves as progressives. He gained local support by advocating an honest and responsive government, freely whipping Tammany to the delight of his rural, Republican-leaning constituency, and grandly exploiting his Roosevelt name. But after an overwhelming defeat in 1914 by an able Tammany candidate in an ill-advised try for the party nomination for the U.S. Senate, Roosevelt made an uneasy peace with Tammany and maintained it for the rest of his career. Without it no Democrat could win state-wide election in New York. Instead of specific policies, Roosevelt relied, whenever possible, on humane sentiment and a vague sympathy for most moderate reform efforts. He tried to keep as broad a political base as possible and to move with popular opinion, as he cleverly did on the aggravating issue of prohibition. He worked assiduously for the best possible publicity. He loved journalism and easily won the sympathy of reporters. Later he condemned publishers in part because they obstructed his own successful efforts to persuade the working press. Personal appeal, plus general promises, was usually enough to win him elections, whereas less persuasive politicians had to rely more on policies. Roosevelt's vagueness was not sheer political tactics but very often reflected his own lack of clarity and his tendency to move with events.

Roosevelt first learned about national politics as Wilson's assistant secretary of the navy, but here again remained aloof from controversial domestic issues. Typically, he exploited his eight years for all possible political gains. Yet, unlike Theodore Roosevelt, he could never find his Manila Bay, or chart any other dramatic course of action to propel him into the presidency. Heaven knows he tried hard enough. He echoed Theodore in demanding a large navy, in general militancy, and in his thirst for imperial glory. He easily accepted, and even abetted, our policy of Caribbean intervention. Frequently close to insubordination to a fatherly and forgiving Josephus Daniels, the navy secretary, he conspired with naval officers and interventionists, urged compulsory military training (a lifelong interest), and always thirsted for a good fight. If his speeches had been able to effect it, he would have had a war out of the Tampico incident with Mexico. A world removed from the peace orientation of William Jennings Bryan, his militancy was eventually rewarded by events, and even his most youthful chauvinism became a national mania. With more enthusiasm than wisdom, he enjoyed the ceremonial duties of his office and rather cavalierly used naval ships for personal pleasure. But, with Howe's aid, he did an able job administering, amid the maximum publicity, the civilian branches of the navy, learning something about production, about labor unions and labor leaders, and about competitive techniques in business. The yardstick justification for limited government ownership came from his navy experiences. With war, his task became frustrating. He wanted desperately to be in the fight and even managed to turn one terribly safe European tour into a grand and romanticized adventure.

Roosevelt's two terms as governor of New York placed him in a national showcase. He was able to put on display some of the later New Deal, even as he calculated policies to boost his ill-concealed presidential hopes for 1932. To his personal assets, to his regained health after polio, to a very professional political organization, he slowly added another requisite for a national leader—a quite general program. Reluctant in areas of controversy, often as carefully ambiguous as possible, he nonetheless identified himself with certain issues. Even before the stock market crash he backed modest state reforms in agriculture, power, and welfare. Always partial to the farmer, concerned with the desperate plight of New York's highly diversified small farms, he worked for tax relief and inaugurated studies on land use. Consistent with a long interest in conservation, conscious of midwestern and western concern, he carefully worked out proposals for a mixed public-private development of the water resources of the St. Lawrence. He wanted close public regulation of utilities, with profits limited to the level of prudent investment and with government ownership as a last resort to insure fair prices. In welfare he worked on prison reform and tried to extend old-age pensions. He did nothing to arrest the great bull market and had no real grasp of what happened in the October crash. Militantly insisting on state rights, he was not even very cooperative in early federal public works programs. As late as 1930 he condemned Hoover's policies as too radical, as contrary to supply and demand, and, in the case of public works, as too big a drain on the treasury.

In his last, depression-conscious term as governor, Roosevelt instituted a minor New Deal for the state. His reelection in 1930 was of landslide proportions, giving him an amenable legislature for the first time. He appeased both sides on prohibition by advocating repeal but insisting upon local option.

He cut the state budget and pressed for economy in all areas of government, but still had to resort to borrowing to meet pressing needs. From a rigid state-rights position, he finally accepted the idea of federal relief aid. As bank failures increased, and particularly after the disastrous failure of the Bank of the United States in December 1930, he cautiously conducted an investigation and pressed for mild financial reforms, but here he still lagged behind President Hoover. In the frustration of securing self-regulation and sincere cooperation from private bankers, he lost some of his earlier faith in their competence and was thus ready to make them whipping boys in 1932.

In New York Roosevelt slowly increased public works and, as a temporary expedient in 1931, set up a Temporary Emergency Relief Administration. Under the able direction of a former social worker, Harry Hopkins (incidentally, not selected by Roosevelt), it distributed over twenty-five million dollars by the election of 1932 and provided relief for 10 percent of the families in the state. In the program, Roosevelt asked for work relief whenever possible (usually it was not). Finally, and most dear to his heart, he tried, with some small success, to get people back to the land. He had great faith in new, carefully planned rural communities, containing part-time agriculture and small industries. These related to his interest in the planned use of land, in reforestation, and in city planning. Here alone, in an area of lifelong interest, his depression policy went beyond expedient reaction to compelling need and embraced a vision, perhaps a hopelessly impractical vision, of a new America.

Thus, by 1932, Roosevelt had executive experience, a growing national reputation, great political artistry, and the outlines of a program. He was confident, self-assured, seemingly undismayed by the magnitude of depression problems, but intellectually vague. With no clear understanding of himself, of economic realities, or even of the hazards that he would soon face, he was still supremely available and appealing. He did not have the substance, the wisdom, for great leadership. He never did. But he had the form, and in 1932 the form seemed more important than the substance.

TWO

Clouds Over a New Era, 1932–1934

The New Deal, as a varied series of legislative acts and executive orders dealing either with the problems of depression or with problems created or aggravated by depression, lasted only five years. Most of the important legislation came in brief spurts in 1933, 1935, and, least important, in 1938. But the volume of important legislation so exceeded any earlier precedents, so overwhelmed the immediate capacity for full comprehension, that even today no one can more than begin to make sense out of the whole.

Most New Deal legislation was, in a broad sense, economic. The early legislation was directed at early economic recovery. Some of it, as well as much later legislation, dealt directly with the overall structure of our market system and with the relationship of the federal government to this system. After 1934 the most significant New Deal measures dealt more directly with the immediate economic needs of individuals, families, or exploited groups. These efforts failed to gain complete recovery but significantly modified the American economy. After the New Deal innovations, major producers enjoyed more security in their property, more certainty of profits, less vulnerability to economic cycles, and both more federal subsidies and more extensive federal regulation. Laborers had clearer rights to organize unions and gained new political leverage in the Democratic party. Finally, new welfare policies guaranteed at least a minimum of subsistence for many people excluded from, or unable to compete effectively for, the benefits of a corporate and highly centralized system of production.

By habit, historians often divide the New Deal into two parts. The identification of a second New Deal goes back to contemporary newspaper articles, which noted a policy shift in 1935 toward welfare legislation and a divisive class appeal. Some major changes did occur in 1935, but they overlay continuities in agricultural policy and in resource management. Also, the crucial Court-packing issue in 1937, and other Roosevelt efforts to attain a more directly responsive democracy, might even lend credence to a third New Deal. But all such categories have an arbitrary aspect and are justified only by their usefulness.

In 1932 Roosevelt asked for only one clear mandate—bold action. In what seemed a terribly dangerous and callous demagoguery to an exasperated Hoover, an unseasoned immaturity to commentators, Roosevelt refused to use his campaign to chart a coherent economic program, with all its demands and costs and promised rewards. In many cases he could not. On the central problem of recovery he was lost, although the outlines of the National Recovery Administration (NRA) and the Agricultural Adjustment Administration (AAA) were already forming.

But even in areas where his commitments were firm, he preferred general to specific recommendations and refused to join Hoover in a serious dialogue either on the causes of the depression or on basic American ideals. He balanced suggestive speeches on forgotten men, concert of interests, planning of production and distribution, administered resources, and restored purchasing power with traditional pledges of a lower budget and complete fiscal integrity. Most of the time he simply berated the Hoover administration, condemned Republican mistakes, or promised to drive the evil money-changers from the temple. His concealed pack seemed to be full of aces, with something for almost everyone but the financiers. Even his devils were vague enough to be almost empty. At times every ambiguous label of the American political repertoire seemed to fit—left or right, liberal or conservative, socialist or capitalist, individualist or collectivist. His technique proved a political success. Even much of the vagueness, much of the ambiguity, was unavoidable. It was Roosevelt, an unbeatable Roosevelt, at work. But, of course, only some of the cards could be played. Many newly aroused hopes could never be fulfilled.

The overwhelming concern of almost everyone in 1933 was recovery, the most attractive but elusive god of the thirties. This was Roosevelt's clearest commitment. If he had quickly attained this goal much of the later New Deal, including the relief and welfare programs, would have seemed unnecessary. For this reason the NRA, with its permissive monopolies in each industry, its elaborate code system, and its fanfare and promotional excesses, was the most important agency established during the famous hundred-day legislative session of 1933. Complementing this was a complex agricultural act, which established the AAA and inaugurated several lasting programs looking toward both recovery and structural changes. These two efforts represented Roosevelt's earliest response to unprecedented economic maladies which he blamed on Hoover and the Republican party.

Herbert Hoover was the most tragic figure in America in 1933. To him, life was not a joyous challenge but a moral pilgrimage. In 1928 he had entertained an optimistic, near utopian vision. Now he had to struggle to maintain the vision, and even more to bring reality back in line with it. Like John Adams in 1800, he felt that he had been right in his policies. He knew that he was far more conscientious than Franklin D. Roosevelt. Further, he felt that Roosevelt endangered the final achievement of his vision by irresponsibly exploiting a temporary setback in behalf of personal power and purely political goals. Hoover was victim in part of an accident of history, in part of his limiting concepts, in part of his nonpolitical outlook, and in part of his very sincerity and deep seriousness. Fate forever dictates that troubled men prefer words of cheer, even if ambiguous, to hard realities, and charismatic heroes, even if vague, to conscientious but unimaginative servants. Hoover vainly tried to make the campaign a debate on vital principles, but with no response. Not that Roosevelt rejected Hoover's principles—he never even seemed to listen to them. In 1932 it was difficult to prove any vital difference of belief.

In America the purportedly free market economy of classical theory had achieved a whole new level of productive output in the twenties. Hoover had acclaimed the feat in 1928. Problems remained, grave moral and social problems. Hoover was blind to all too many of these but wanted to cure others. The purely economic weaknesses seemed minor in comparison to the productive achievement. Hoover noted fiscal ills and nagging problems of distribution, both of which he wanted to correct. Finally, he always argued that the most serious weaknesses were foreign-based but important to the United States because they involved its proportionately small but marginally vital international trade.

The twenties, instead of representing a vast, delusive economic bubble as so often suggested by popular historians, pointed to almost infinite economic possibilities in America. Overall growth was rapid. New tools, both in management and technology, developed at unprecedented rates. Numerous corporate consolidations increased efficiency even as they narrowed participation in key managerial choices. The private sectors, including even agriculture, realized the possibilities of credit (if politicians had realized that the government could buy economic growth on the installment plan, there might have been no serious depression). Even high prices on common stock, at least until the final speculative mania of 1928–1929, were high in relation to earnings but quite reasonable in light of plausible growth potential. The depression resulted, not from false prosperity (it was real in every way, although not equally shared), but from a lack of sufficient economic knowledge and political wisdom to apply needed medicine—preventive before 1929 or, more crucial still, curative from 1929 through the whole decade of the thirties.

The depression was not a failure of the twenties, but an affliction of the thirties. Measures in the twenties sufficient to have averted the subsequent depression would not only have risked an earlier economic collapse because of their psychological impact, but also were politically impossible because they would have required so many hated restraints on prospering people. The cure almost had to come after the collapse. And both Hoover and Roosevelt tried, to the best of their ability, to find and apply a cure. Both failed. It is even arguable that their various medicines, often working at cross purposes to each other, even prolonged the depression by suppressing natural recovery. In the absence of an early cure, Hoover, and even more Roosevelt, tried to alleviate some of the attendant suffering. Both presidents could also point to temporary economic gains. Briefly in early 1937, most economic indexes (save for employment) surpassed the 1929 level, but a second disastrous spiral of declines scarcely allowed Roosevelt time to celebrate his apparent achievement. These economic reverses, which tragically documented a general lack of economic knowledge among politicians, meant that the United States sacrificed a large share of its productive potential for over a decade. Plants, tools, people remained idle, with untold effects that reach all the way down to the present.

A market economy is one in which private choices determine investment, production, prices, and wages. Unless given an impossibly narrow definition, a market system does not necessitate laissez-faire, a near meaningless, largely emotive term by the twentieth century. Always, to an extent never realized by some classical economists, public policy provides the matrix of economic transactions, even to the extent of legitimatizing private choice in any given area. In the most free situation, government secures property rights, grants corporate charters, taxes for community needs, provides a currency system, and may intervene directly to keep the area of choice as free and open as possible. Even by the twenties, internal controls in highly collective enterprises had so lowered the range of choice as to threaten the very idea of a free market.

The most permissive market developed in the nineteenth century, and with it came rapid growth but, at the same time, internal tendencies toward monopoly. Free trade or low tariffs allowed the market to encompass all advanced industrial states, creating more potential for growth through specialization but a great deal more international dependency. Cycles of boom and bust, seemingly endemic to a permissive system, were either survived (America) or the most inhumane results alleviated by welfare measures (Europe). Through political control, or simply by technological advantages and aggressive trade efforts, western countries transferred a share of the burden of rapid capital accumulation to underdeveloped countries or colonies. Meanwhile, labor unions allowed more and more skilled and able workers to bargain effectively for higher wages (and thus further limit individual choice). In America an acquisitive, egoistic desire for private accumulation, a major motive for economic expansion, was often restrained by an ingrained sense of community responsibility on the part of industrial managers and, much more important, by their slowly developing recognition that stable growth is a more potent and reliable source of profits than callous exploitation and that both cannot exist together for a long period.

This was the "glorious" but evolving system Hoover acclaimed in 1928. He wanted improvements. At the private level, he desired an even greater sense of community responsibility, a fully moralized as well as rationalized marketplace. Hence his appeals to various groups and his pathetic reliance on persuasion and moral lectures even after 1929. He wanted private decisions to be made in behalf of a broader conception of private ends—that is, in terms of the individual as part of the group. If all corporate managers could have been as generous and humane as Hoover, and a bit more perceptive, his dream might have been possible. Roosevelt also tried Hoover's type of persuasion but quickly gave up. Yet, instead of disciplining unrepentant private groups, he often was content merely to berate them.

At the public level Hoover repudiated any lingering laissez-faire nonsense but still acclaimed free choice. Laissez-faire meant acquiescence, when he wanted governmental responsibility. The state could hasten the glorious era of abundance. It had to discipline the sinful, aid the righteous, provide the mechanisms of a fair and stable market, and broaden the opportunities for all. But government, a tool of private choice, should not make the most crucial decisions, even under a broad mandate like Roosevelt's in 1933. Hoover feared a regimented, subsidized, regulated society. Even if it did maintain prosperity (he doubted the possibility), it would dehumanize man, inevitably create a narrow, bureaucratic elite, and turn democracy into periodic, ritualistic plebiscites to enthrone demagogues.

But how to get back on the highroad to abundance with freedom? Trying never to violate freedom, facing a hostile Congress, Hoover did everything possible consistent with his values. This was never nearly enough. He faced insurmountable odds. His humanized, capitalist utopia, like so many others, was a chimera. Possibly his dream was out of date, or perhaps it never fit reality. By 1929 the international market was pinned up by American credit and imperiled by trade barriers and nonliberal ideologies. In 1931 it collapsed, like Humpty Dumpty, never to be put together again. Back of 1931 lay Versailles, and beyond that the 1914 climax of imperial clashes over exploitable markets. The best were gone by 1914; after the thirties the best would no longer submit to exploitation. A free

American market could not survive without a free and prosperous international market. This Hoover sensed and committed his country, insofar as political realities permitted and in the same way that he wanted to commit all good businessmen, to larger than personal or national goals. In Hoover, Wilson was resurrected as an economist, and went forth to save the market in behalf of free man. Thus Hoover's moratorium on the war debts, his zealous commitment to a preserved gold standard and international liquidity, his fear of monetary inflation, his hopes for the 1933 London Economic Conference, his desperate efforts to get Roosevelt to come to some economic agreement immediately after the election. He knew that his utopia could not be born in a world of selfish nations and enslaved people, that recovery, in terms of his vision, could not take place in island America. At home, recovery could parallel recovery in Europe only if we honored the venerable ethics of the marketplace.

Hoover was clear; he was also wrong. A well-intentioned man, he played out his tragedy to the bitter end and then let it almost destroy him, for bitterness engulfed and warped the disillusioned man that survived. In his place came Roosevelt, with his flashing smile and nice slogans and gay optimism. He came to rescue America from Republican sins and never doubted his ability to do just that. The New Deal was already in the oven, only half-baked, but it had to be served quickly. It was avidly greeted, even by many who soon detested it. Yet, in spite of their growing lament, the sick economy looked less pale and almost justified the illusion of near miraculous recovery. Perhaps all it had needed was a bit of Roosevelt's good cheer to wash down some queer-tasting alphabetical soup. Actually, there was nothing to fear but fear itself. All the Republican windmills gave way, and the heavens cheered.

The setting of the inauguration in 1933 was perfect for a hero. Depression, bank panic, fear, the darkness could not deepen. No dramatist could have plotted a more desolate and appropriate scene for a hero's entry. The situation invited a surrender of power to some leader. Everyone was willing to give Roosevelt an opportunity to work his magic. He had the most anxious and willing Congress in our history. Almost any legislative proposal would pass. But, again, the realities of the situation invite continued controversy.

Next to the Court-packing issue, Roosevelt's actions during the long interregnum (November 1932 to March 1933) are hardest to understand and defend. Hoover was absolutely helpless, repudiated and soul sick. After the election he approached Roosevelt about foreign economic issues. Concerned about the European war debts, personally committed to debt reduction and postponed payments as a generous aid to European recovery, he wanted Roosevelt at least to cooperate in choosing delegates to a new commission to explore the debt problem. Later, he tried to get Roosevelt to join in plans for the upcoming London Economic Conference, then scheduled for the spring of 1933. Back of his desire to confer with Roosevelt was his private certainty that the depression could be cured only by international efforts. At two famous meetings, Roosevelt, lost in the array of facts and figures, incapable of understanding the intricacies of Hoover's ideas, fearful of a trap that would limit his later freedom of action, aware of the political dangers of cancellation, and possibly sensing (Tugwell attests to this) that debt adjustment would aid immoral international bankers, not only refused to cooperate, but was at his vague, bland, enigmatic best. After the first strained meeting, Hoover despaired of any salvation for America and fretted while Roosevelt went on a highly publicized vacation, leaving his "brain trust" to work feverishly on legislative proposals. Thus, very early, and without a conscious choice, Roosevelt began to sabotage Hoover's dream of an honest and generous America coming to the aid of European governments. Roosevelt at least temporarily rejected the old Wilsonian internationalism. If he had been more honest and straightforward, this decision was defensible, possibly even brilliant. It was probably too late to shore up Western European economies, and it was at least debatable whether they deserved shoring up.

After January 1 the whole financial system began to collapse, with the depression rapidly worsening. As more and more banks failed, the whole economic system faced complete, immobilizing anarchy. Hoover, without power to act decisively, convinced that the bank crisis flowed in part from the fear created among investors by many of Roosevelt's campaign statements and by the general uncertainty about future policies, wrote a desperate note to Roosevelt in February, apprising him of the severity of the crisis and pleading for help in arresting it. But instead of simply asking for some statement to allay fear, Hoover provided the exact and completely unacceptable content of such a statement—a promise by Roosevelt not to tamper with the currency, unbalance the budget, or impair government credit. Roosevelt ignored the letter (lamely explaining later that his reply had been misplaced), did nothing, and helplessly watched the economy collapse, letting it appear as one last result of Republican incompetence. He refused last-minute pleas from Hoover that the two men join in asking for a bank holiday.

Roosevelt surely had better alternatives than those proffered by Hoover. Any assumption of responsibility, any promised policies (including the emergency banking act already being drafted and to be passed just after the inauguration), might have helped alleviate the panic and lessen the fear that existed by March 4. It seemed to cynical critics that Roosevelt wanted the worst possible setting for his own beginnings. Yet he was not so callous as to play with the fortunes of millions of small depositors for purely political reasons. Roosevelt possibly never grasped the immense human suffering involved or honestly did not know what he could do about the situation. Politically, the situation was perfect. The crisis of 1933 was a sharp ravine in the broad valley of depression. Even though the mountain of recovery was far ahead, the ravine could be quickly scaled by the same banking policies that could have prevented it. Thus, Roosevelt could launch his administration on a note of quick, positive, and successful action.

Friendly historians have almost universally defended both Roosevelt's inaction and his refusal to cooperate on Hoover's terms. The soon well-established image of Hoover's ineptness, and the prominence given to Hoover's efforts to entrap Roosevelt, helped divert attention from possible areas of independent action. Embittered critics of the American economic system, such as Marxists, rejoiced in the economic chaos. At the other extreme, Hoover used the nice advantage of hindsight to make an elaborate and impressive defense of his own "unselfish" position and to denounce an incompetent, callous Roosevelt, who for political reasons deliberately permitted and abetted the final and complete economic collapse, even as international recovery was already well under way. Thus, to Hoover, the long depression of the New Deal period was an unnecessary, Democratic depression.

Although able to cure the banking crisis, Roosevelt could not find the needed magic for early recovery. He, like almost all Americans, was pathetically ill-equipped to face the hard realities that awaited his administration. Among the advising professors, both Rexford G. Tugwell and Adolf Berle were competent economists and at least aware of many of the difficulties awaiting any thorough economic reconstruction. Tugwell wanted to bludgeon ahead and do what was necessary, regardless of the cost in discipline, coercion of the unwilling, and lost votes. But he underestimated the political impediments. He could never quite penetrate the conventional beliefs that pre- vented Roosevelt from grasping the complexity and difficulty of economic problems. Thus even Roosevelt, magical persuader that he was, probably could not have persuaded the people to accept any extreme recovery measures. Opinion polls as late as 1939 showed less than 20 percent of Americans willing to accept such mild expedients as unbalanced federal budgets. In this sense, Roosevelt was as captive to events and to ancient verities as Hoover, despite all his political flexibility. But he made a better game out of it and never suffered the personal despair. In fact, as with his polio, he never accepted his own limitations and kept looking for a full cure, claiming progress day by day.

Hoover had been correct on one issue. Confidence is a very important ingredient in a market economy. It was totally lacking in 1933. Roosevelt's campaign failed to inspire much of it among corporation executives, whose decisions were all-important in sparking recovery, or among those in the middle class who had not suffered drastic losses and had savings to spend or invest but who chose to wait. No one can say for sure, but an avowedly probusiness administration in 1933, with a relatively small amount of aid to producers, might have encouraged a spiral of recovery, but recovery without significant reform and without safeguards against future depressions. The recovery during World War II came through what amounted to an enormous government subsidy to private business.

Corporate executives, like almost everyone else, are usually captives of their own mythical world view. In 1933 theirs was unbelievably restrictive and matched their own insecurity and loss of popularity. Relatively orthodox policies frightened them and led to fantastic but sincere charges of radicalism and government collectivism. A New Deal frankly committed to higher profits, to stable prices, to a better banking and investment system, to regressive taxes aimed at the income and savings of low- and middle-income groups, and to some increased spending for business subsidies and minimal public welfare might have brought the elusive confidence that was so lacking. Ironically, contrary to most intentions and expectations, the whole body of New Deal legislation would lead to just such results.

The early New Deal seemed to have a larger treat for corporations than for any other economic interest. As first administered, the NRA proved a wonderful gift, with its paternal blessings upon unencumbered business self-regulation. But Roosevelt tried to be an honest broker and thus responded to other clients. He refused to enlist as a demanding ally of business or, even better for them, to become a compliant tool. His gifts had strings attached, although not very specific ones in 1933. Prodded by his brain trust, Roosevelt talked of public goals as conditions for his concessions to business and made gestures toward both laborers and consumers. This was different, or at least sounded different, from Hoover's sermons on public responsibility. It was one thing to be reminded that businessmen are servants of mankind, and another to be told that the government would make them serve mankind. Besides, could a businessman really trust Roosevelt? Soon the Tennessee Valley Authority posed the specter of government ownership. He was not very kind to utility companies. And how could he pay for all the new programs? Most horrible, look at what he was doing with the dollar, and with that standard of all value, gold. The caveats could go on for pages.

The National Industrial Recovery Act (NIRA) actually provided two main mechanisms of recovery. Roosevelt placed the first, public works, in the Department of the Interior, under Harold Ickes. A much more imaginative man than usually conceded, Ickes required careful planning of projects, jealously guarded against waste and political influence, and eventually secured the maximum benefits from always too limited funds. His successful Public Works Administration (PWA) soon allocated over three billion dollars, but the actual construction proceeded too slowly to have any drastic effect on recovery. Here, the New Deal simply expanded the even more cautious public works program of the Hoover administration.

The NRA, on the other hand, represented a vast potential, either for the imposition of central economic plans upon private corporations, for a government-protected business commonwealth, or for a better-regulated atmosphere for open and fair competition. Each of these possibilities had able advocates in the Roosevelt administration, and each struggled for control of the early NRA. The planners, such as Tugwell, never had a chance and lost most battles. The NRA never really tried, in any extensive or coherent way, to force public goals upon an unwilling business community. It was the businessmen who dominated the early NRA, both in the writing of codes and in the operation of the enforcing code authorities. Usually without direct price setting, most industry codes achieved the same result indirectly by limiting production, preventing price cutting, and forbidding unfair competition. Labor and consumer representatives almost never had voting rights on the code authorities. Even the lone government representative usually reflected a business outlook and thus rarely used his veto power. But the advocates of competition, concerned about the fate of small business or consumers, soon provided an effective counterforce and eventually enacted some antimonopolistic modifications in NRA policies.

Hugh Johnson, the flamboyant first administrator of the NRA, tried to enlist voluntary cooperation from corporate leaders and was therefore quite reluctant to impose governmental restrictions. In a fanfare of publicity, featuring a celebrated Blue Eagle, Johnson secured almost unanimous participation in early, precode reemployment agreements. The later industrial codes, drafted by hundreds of industries, usually ended anarchic competition, increased efficiency, and in some areas temporarily increased employment. But they also raised prices, limited production, narrowed the leeway of some small businesses, and failed to produce any general recovery. The vast number of codes, the lack of specific governmental mandates, and a reluctance to antagonize business leaders prevented strict enforcement. Many corporations evaded the labor codes (bargaining rights, wage-hour protection, prevention of child labor) required by Section 7(a) of the NIRA, either by establishing company unions or by deliberate refusals to recognize legitimate unions.

The NRA, bereft of clear policy guidelines from Roosevelt, slowly achieved a new equilibrium between business desires for legal but selfish collusion and the old, symbolically powerful gospel of competition. Before the NRA, the collusion had been selective and clandestine; now, briefly, it was general and open. But the NRA codes invited the concerted opposition, not only of those who genuinely feared monopoly, hated bigness, and loved consumers, but of all who were disgruntled with the actual operations of the NRA. These critics scrutinized the codes, endlessly and critically investigated the NRA, forced Johnson out, and pressured the NRA toward more circumspect, consumer-oriented codes and more scrupulous enforcement by code authorities. With personnel changes, government representatives became more independent and demanding. More and more businessmen became disillusioned with the NRA. A few independent mavericks, like Henry Ford, resisted from the beginning. Others resented the labor provisions, reacted to internal wrangling, or felt cheated by the operation of the codes. Even the business opposition hid behind the symbol of free competition. After the Supreme Court declared the codes unconstitutional in 1935, many businessmen gladly went back to clandestine collusion, happy to be rid of legal cooperation under the glare of unfavorable publicity and with an ever present threat of unhelpful government interference. But Congress, in new specialized legislation, tried to bring supervised order to several highly competitive industries.

Roosevelt's emphasis upon the NRA, and upon a degree of cooperation with business, was not necessarily a betrayal of the expectations of the army of would-be reformers that rushed to Washington, although it seemed so to many of the old progressives. But the NRA had to justify itself in rapid recovery. Even with all its resented inequities, the economy in the twenties had offered more for almost every class and group than did the economy in the thirties. Any preference for the thirties had to rest on other than economic rewards—on a sense of community created by adversity, on feeble attempts to create economic democracy through cooperation, on more equity for, if not in, agriculture, on alleviative welfare measures for the suffering, or even on the pervasive sense of optimism that gripped American leftists. Regardless of New Deal welfare programs, the main burden of depression, the tremendous waste of human resources, fell more heavily on the poor than on the rich. Thus, a new deal for America had to bring recovery or be a vast delusion. Yet, despite all of Hugh Johnson's heroic efforts, recovery never came through the initiative of private business leaders. Some advisers, such as Rexford Tugwell, did not mind. They wanted to clear the way for new governmental programs that would not only bring recovery but would also reform the economic system in behalf of fair returns to all and the final elimination of privilege based on private selfishness.

Tugwell is often considered the architect of the first New Deal. He may have drawn the plans, but they certainly were never implemented. An institutional economist, he wanted major structural changes both in government and in the economy. He welcomed the centralizing trends in business and praised new managerial techniques as highly as new technology. He hated "progressivism," which he defined as a rural, Jeffersonian attempt to atomize and fragment the economy. His term "concert of interests" meant a collective, cooperative system, without divisive private interests. The collective tendencies, already irresistible in business, should have been allowed to culminate in one unified nation, not in a few large, powerful, selfish corporations or unions. The controls and central planning of World War I seemed an unfulfilled promise, which he had hoped finally to implement by such an agency as the NRA. Guided by expert planners, disciplined by long-range economic goals, the government should make the important management decisions for the whole economy and not be content to act as a mere referee. Allocation of resources, priorities in production, profits, wages, prices—all should be determined by government in behalf of the whole nation, not the more powerful or persuasive interest groups. As under the old market system, consumer choice, private ownership, and limited entrepreneurial decisions would remain, but not private decisions affecting the whole economy. Like Berle, he felt that management, not ownership, had to be socialized and moralized and thus advocated nationalization only when private industries refused to fulfill public goals. He rejected all minimal types of government interference, such as purely fiscal measures, because he did not want a revivified private market and all the injustices that he identified with it even in times of prosperity.

Tugwell pointed the way to recovery, but at what cost? Even in the most persuasive language of Roosevelt, Tugwell's ideas still sounded heretical. Tugwell believed the vaunted freedom of our economic system had become freedom for a very few, just as Berle and Gardiner C. Means had demonstrated that property had lost almost all its original managerial prerogatives. In a managed economy, despite guidance from planners (corporate executives utilized them all the time), a vast majority of the people could enjoy a broader participation and fairer returns. But a few would lose their existing freedom and much of their existing income. So be it; this was the reality of any significant reform, made all the more dangerous politically because the resisting groups were the most powerful in the country. In Tugwell there were faint echoes of technocracy, a hint of a corporate state, and a near arrogant contempt for such traditional values as competition, small economic units, and fee simple property. His policies suggested enough varied controls to frighten almost everyone. Also, from an economic standpoint, Tugwell knew that the threat of government controls (planning, as Tugwell used the term, really meant positive controls) would lower business confidence and further disrupt the already low level of private initiative. This required, for quick recovery, a great deal more regimentation than ever dreamed of in World War I. Roosevelt, fascinated with a milder form of planning (advisory rather than positive controls), probably never grasped, let alone accepted, the full implications of Tugwell's centralized economy. If he did, he knew that it was politically explosive. As Tugwell conceded, Roosevelt could not be induced to think and act outside of a political context.

If not planning, but only a few gestures toward planning, if not an alliance with business, but only a few resented gifts, then the New Deal seemed to have only monetary and fiscal avenues left—changes in the value or supply of money, or shifts in taxation or the level of government spending. Of course, eventually, these strategies prevailed, at some real cost in surrendered options.

In 1933 a favorite explanation of the depression, at least among New Dealers, was underconsumption. Actually, underconsumption, as well as the other side of the coin, overproduction, were symptoms of economic ills, not causes. Back of both was either a lack of purchasing power or, among those with the means, a psychological unwillingness to purchase. Although in 1932 the later basic ideas of Keynes were known by American economists, anticipated by a New Dealer, Marriner Eccles, and, according to Moley and Tugwell, even broached to Roosevelt in their briefing sessions, Roosevelt never quite accepted the desirability of massive borrowing and, until 1935, had few advisers who did. Yet Roosevelt talked often about restored purchasing power. Since he directed much of this concern at farmers, he primarily meant some method of propping agricultural prices, or else some manipulation of the dollar in order to induce higher prices.

Farmers were demonstrably unhappy even in the twenties. They successfully nourished the myth of a long-term agricultural depression, and thereby provided the very keystone of the Democratic indictment of callous Republican administrations in the twenties. According to the myth, the Republican failure to come to the aid of farmers helped create the decreased spending and reduced purchasing power that did so much to insure a depression after the market crash of 1929. The reality never matched the myth. Overall farm prices in the twenties remained close (within 90 percent) to parity, or to the levels of the prosperous base period of 1909–1914. Farm income increased steadily after the depression of 1921–1922. But all farmers did not share in the moderate prosperity, and almost none realized the profits of the lush war years. Prices in some commodities fluctuated rapidly because of changed consumer demand or international surpluses. The tractor and other new tools placed an ever greater premium on large capital investment, the prudent use of credit, and on expert techniques, all of which penalized the smallest farmers. As usual, severe droughts caused regional distress. Finally, farmers gained new effectiveness in political organization, and thus worked through farm-state congressmen to dramatize their problems and to mute their economic successes.

The myth of continuous depression rested on some hard realities. Although efficient, well-capitalized farms prospered, and able farmers enjoyed living standards above city workers, average farm income remained lower than in any other major occupational grouping. Overall statistics encompassed millions of small, submarginal or inefficient farm units that contributed very little to agricultural production, and were, in fact, scarcely part of an increasingly sophisticated industry. In addition, millions of sharecroppers and farm laborers lived at the very margin of subsistence. The whole course of agricultural development, in both the twenties and thirties, would lead to more and more redundant labor or stranded and hopeless rural families, particularly in the South. Because of unemployment, and ever greater demands for skills, it was both futile and inhumane to ask such farm families to move to the cities and also a mockery of well-established beliefs in the benefits of farm life. Thus, even before 1929, there were grave social problems in rural America, problems not cured but simply concealed by the subsequent migration of desperate rural people to the cities. These under-consuming groups did have a depressing effect on the whole economy. But the exploited rural poor had no voice in the crusade by farm organizations for government-insured price supports in the twenties, and would have received few benefits from such government patronage had the Republicans supported it. They would also gain very little from New Deal agricultural programs, which came in response to the now desperate but still effective demands of formerly prosperous farmers.

The stock market crash of 1929 led almost immediately to a severe drop in farm prices. Agriculture led all other industries into depression, and suffered the most. In 1930 alone, farm income dropped by 20 percent and then by another 30 percent in 1931. Because of complex effects upon international trade and payments balances, the crash forced European countries to cut American imports, and this especially meant a lost market for key farm commodities. For such heavy export crops as tobacco, cotton, and wheat, this meant domestic surpluses and drastic price decreases (cotton from 20¢ a pound in 1927 to only 9¢ in 1930; wheat from $1.19 a bushel to only 67¢). The most able farmers, with large capital investment and mortgage debts, often suffered the most, and they were the very farmers best equipped to translate their grievances into political leverage. They were now in the position of providing a nation's food and fiber at prices well below production costs (industrial prices, and thus the prices for what they had to buy, held almost stable into 1931). Many farmers lost their farms, and by 1933 almost all faced that dismal prospect. Angry at their failure to get relief under the Hoover administration, they had pushed their bitterness to the verge of revolutionary protest. Roosevelt, with his lifelong affinity for farmers, had a heartfelt concern for their suffering, and was astute enough as a politician to respond to their political demands.

But what could be done? The old answers—monetary inflation, extra credit, marketing cooperatives, tariff protection —were either antiquated or almost useless in 1933. Most of the new proposals—acreage control, price adjustments, land retirement—could better the relative position of farmers but only, it seemed, at some risk to overall recovery. For example, the government could fix farm prices and let the consumer, under one or another mechanism, pay the bill. Similarly, by acreage or market controls, or large-scale land retirement, the consumer might be forced to pay higher prices by the operation of the market. But either technique would draw funds from all consumers and penalize low-income urban groups. Obviously it would take from Peter to pay Paul, cutting consumption in one area to pay producers in another, probably decreasing consumption fully as much among consumers as a whole as it increased the purchases of farmers. The first Agricultural Adjustment Act did just this.

This act grew out of a remarkable potpourri of farm-relief proposals developed in the twenties. An omnibus bill, it authorized almost any program desired by the administration. It permitted a limited land retirement program, allowed price-setting marketing agreements between farmers and processors, and allowed a subsidized export program for surplus commodities, or strategies actually used by the new AAA. But another program soon affected more farmers and became the trademark of the AAA. Cooperating farmers in several basic crops, by voluntary contractual agreement, reduced production in return for sufficient government payments to provide prices as close to parity as possible. The payments came from taxes on processing companies, and thus amounted to an indirect sales tax on consumers. Additional legislation in 1934 made mandatory the acreage controls on tobacco and cotton. The AAA received the active support of large farm organizations. With more idealism than immediate success, the actual operation of the program was placed in the hands of local committeemen, who helped persuade farmers to "sign up" and also determined, fairly or unfairly, the allotments and the base for the payments.

The processing tax provision of the Agricultural Adjustment Act was invalidated by the Supreme Court early in 1936. Under new legislation in 1936, the AAA (the agency was not dissolved by the decision) substituted conservation payments drawn directly from the federal treasury. Its policies of acreage reduction and artificial prices would long remain at the heart of government agricultural programs. The AAA brought benefits to almost all commercial farmers. But in limiting acreage and providing the strongest possible incentive for more efficient land use, and thus for better technology, it forced sharecroppers off the land and worsened the plight of farm laborers. It also bypassed harassed farmers in several minor crops and, basing payments on production instead of need, inevitably aided most generously the already large and prospering farmers. Even the grass-roots principle invited all types of local chicanery and too often reinforced class and racial injustice, while the idea of enforced scarcity horrified many urban consumers.

Another enduring agricultural program involved direct government price controls. In a minor way, this began in the fall of 1933 by means of an executive order. The Reconstruction Finance Corporation (RFC) established a farm subsidiary, the Commodity Credit Corporation (one of two New Deal CCCs), which loaned money directly to farmers on the security of their crops. By authorizing loans that exceeded existing prices, and assuming all risks involved, Roosevelt used the CCC to place supports under farm prices. Reminiscent of the old warehouse receipt plan of the Farmers' Alliance, this began the support, storage, and marketing adventure of the federal government. Severe droughts rescued the early program from surpluses. Also, everyone at first thought that acreage and marketing controls could keep competitive prices above the support level during most of the year, easily permitting government disposal without loss and possibly with additional income to the farmer. The CCC guarantees were entirely tied to prices and thus to production. They might have been based in part on need and thus have involved a type of intra-agricultural redistribution. As it was, they helped improve the position of agriculture but, like the AAA payments, did little to alleviate injustices within it.

The two principal recovery agencies—the NRA and AAA —provided extra income for the very groups which often seemed least inclined to spend. Both passed the burden of higher prices on to consumers. The mounting reserves of corporations, the conservative savings of salaried workers, the frugal hoardings of AAA payments by cautious farmers, surely contained enough unused wealth to more than restore the economy of the twenties. Empty factories and hungry laborers awaited its reemployment. In addition, banks sought borrowers, while the federal government had vast, unused credit potentialities.

Either tax revision or deficit government spending might have forced the needed economic activity. Roosevelt and most of his advisers opposed large deficits. This left only tax revision. But large tax cuts, which would have encouraged private spending, warred against Roosevelt's commitment to economy and balanced budgets. By more progressive taxes, Roosevelt might have dislodged unused savings from the affluent, but any threat of economic leveling seemed sure to have a disastrous psychological effect upon private initiative. Large wealth does not surrender easily. To have worked at all, such leveling policies would have required either the detailed government controls desired by Tugwell or some form of government ownership, solutions much too radical for Roosevelt, horrifying to Congress, and probably frightening to a vast majority of Americans.

Despite the political perils, Tugwell wanted to force the leveling. Under federal direction, he believed existing wealth was sufficient to underwrite not only recovery but undreamed-of affluence. Deficit spending, at best, was a strategy. Government debts should not be allowed to divert the government from implementing the equalizing features and the controls. To Tugwell, and to most American institutional economists, the danger of deficits without structural changes was the retention of the existing inequities in the system. Their approach was predicated on moral ends, such as justice and fairness, and only secondarily on economic goals. Here, in rough form, was the essential difference between advisers like Tugwell and later followers of Keynes. Tugwell was first of all a moral philosopher and derivatively an economist. The Keynesians often developed more technical finesse as economists but rarely had Tugwell's philosophical breadth, moral sensitivity, or sense of alienation from the existing system.

In retrospect, full recovery seemed impossible for Roosevelt in 1933 and 1934. His diverse political support made impossible any real alliance with business on business terms. Raymond Moley, alone among academic advisers, desired such cooperation. Neither Roosevelt nor the American people desired extensive planning or massive government spending. Thus, as a small NRA boom reversed in late 1933, Roosevelt resorted to a pseudosolution—monetary inflation. To the applause of ghostly greenbackers and populists, he took the United States off the gold standard, stopped gold shipments abroad, propped the price of silver (a vast subsidy to western silver interests), and finally began lowering the gold content of the dollar (or raising the dollar price of gold). The break with gold freed our currency from an old incubus and provided a needed leeway for banking and currency controls and for artificial price fixing in the NRA and AAA. Currency devaluation is a desperate but essential means of correcting a foreign trade imbalance based on overly high prices at home or excessive tariff barriers abroad. But Roosevelt had a quite different goal—artificially higher prices at home. His monetary inflation bore largely bitter fruit. It increased credit when no one wanted to borrow and improved America's foreign trade position when all too few wanted American products. At best, domestic prices rose only slightly, and even then to the despair of consumers. Debtors and small producers did not benefit. Neither was large wealth penalized; just horrified. Adversely, the almost halved dollar in effect raised the tariff by nearly 50 percent (by the change in the rate of exchange) and thus helped bolster a wall of economic nationalism. It made a mockery of earlier Democratic criticism of the Smoot-Hawley tariff, a mockery only slowly relieved by Cordell Hull's patient work in behalf of reciprocal trade treaties.

It was Roosevelt's early but unannounced plans for his manipulation of gold that led to his unexpected about-face during the 1933 London Economic Conference. His bombshell message, reneging on earlier promises and announcing his refusal to back any plan for currency stabilization, wrecked the conference and, with it, the hopes of British and French governments for more favorable trade relations with the United States. The London conference came at the dramatic end of a whole epoch of Western Civilization. Well-publicized, supported by ill-founded hopes, it seemed a last, desperate bid for stable commerce, freer trade, and interdependent national economies. Also, it was a last attempt to maintain a western economic system that, by superior technology and masterful diplomacy, had managed to develop and exploit most of the world. The tasks of the conference were stupendous and surely impossible, but the effort had great symbolic value. In the view of Raymond Moley, a participant, Roosevelt completely bungled the affair by reversing himself, betraying his own delegates, misleading other countries, and revealing his ignorance of the principal issues involved.

Even Roosevelt locked one group out of his honeymoon suite. The financiers, the reckless promoters of campaign rhetoric, were the prime devils of almost everyone. Even Hoover placed much of the blame for the stock market crash on speculation and poor banking ethics. Thus, while Hugh Johnson was wooing big corporations, Roosevelt won plaudits from old progressives by doing battle with Wall Street. His effort, however much committed to the old dream of fair and equal competition, dramatically improved the central fiscal mechanism of the country. The Emergency Banking Act, drafted by Hoover bureaucrats and passed almost immediately in the new Congress, provided for inspections and certification of soundness and may have prevented a state banking system. The Glass-Steagall Act provided for Federal Reserve regulation of bank investments, forced the separation of investment and commercial banking, and created a Federal Depositors Insurance Corporation to insure small depositors, all of which strengthened banks and gave protection to the most innocent depositors.

In the same way the Securities Act of 1933 forced the most fraudulent promoters out of the stock market and required more detailed accounting by stock-issuing corporations. The Securities and Exchange Act of 1934 set up the Securities and Exchange Commission (SEC) to regulate trading practices and to force full disclosure of information, and permitted the Federal Reserve Board to regulate margin requirements on stock purchases. Then, in 1934, after Roosevelt gave up on inflation, the Gold Reserve Act restored a stable currency at a depreciated level. These stabilizing policies had long been desired by mature manufacturing and farming interests. But attempts, particularly by Tugwell, to get modifications in other than the money and securities market met with complete failure. He lost a long and futile battle for an effective food and drug act in behalf of consumers and directed against the more unethical advertising and labeling policies of manufacturers and retailers.

In the first two years of the New Deal, Roosevelt persuaded a compliant Congress to enact several of his campaign commitments. The old devil prohibition was quickly routed by a beer bill and the hasty repeal of the Eighteenth Amendment. His long-time support for a back-to-the-land movement resulted in the Division of Subsistency Homesteads (created in the Department of the Interior by authority of a subsection of the NIRA) and in a community program initiated by a rural division of the Federal Emergency Relief Administration (FERA). His promise of government economy led to the Economy Act of 1933, passed just after the Emergency Banking Act. Unimportant, even

'not always good industry) and surely helped
standards in parts of the valley, with TVA
too much credit for the growth. Despite
ver the allocation of appropriated funds, the
efficiency, flexibility, and social concern
rnment-owned, nonprofit corporations. Of all
ms, the TVA had the most impact on foreign

essional elections of 1934, the first phase of the
ver. Most of the legislation came in 1933. The
helming, confusing, chaotic. Roosevelt fulfilled
action, but could not provide clear direction.
intense suffering still haunted the land. Most
s in 1934 remained as low as in 1931. In fact,
l product only reached the 1931 level in 1936.
one could find something to approve as well as
ose. No one could make sense of the whole. No
oosevelt, knew everything taking place in the
ngressmen were often completely oblivious of
programs. But at the political level, as the 1934
s proved, Roosevelt was more popular than
ayed well the game of morale building, had
to millions by fireside chats, and still infused a
nce. He loved his office and easily fit his varied

of the New Deal was not at the level of political
dden in the agencies and subagencies. Roose-
re to pursue one coherent program allowed a
of fascinating people to enter the government
them were the social workers and do-gooders, a
ademies but most from labor unions, welfare
apers, and architectural firms. They were often
New Deal, molded more in the humane image of
elt than that of her politician husband. Some
even utopian dreamers. They were often as
as Roosevelt was conventional, as dogmatic in
as flexible, as cocksure of their own plans as he

ironical in later perspective, the reduction in federal salaries and veterans' bonuses truly represented Roosevelt's desire for a balanced budget. Roosevelt always distinguished between general expenditures, which he tried to reduce, and emergency expenditures, which he reluctantly authorized according to pressing needs. Beyond the temporary emergency, which he often described in the rhetoric of war, he hoped to achieve a balanced budget in part as a result of many small economies. He almost achieved it, for a moment, in 1937.

More important, Roosevelt fulfilled his promise of additional relief. He brought Harry Hopkins to Washington to head a new FERA, which expanded Hoover's cautious relief program through larger, supervised grants to the states. In behalf of Roosevelt's old goal of work relief, and to help the most desperate families through the cruel winter of 1933–1934, Hopkins also directed a temporary, poorly planned, politically vulnerable but humane program, the Civil Works Administration (CWA), which employed over four million people in minor construction or even in "made" work.

In all the confusion of New Deal policy, one theme endured from beginning to end. In the broad area of resource management, Roosevelt was clear and consistent. He wanted conservation and planned land use. On this he never equivocated and compromised only when he had to. Thus the Civilian Conservation Corps (CCC) was ever close to his heart. Young men received employment, military discipline (Roosevelt desired that), and at the same time improved and beautified our forest resources. This early version of a domestic Peace Corps worked well despite unbelievable administrative complexity. Likewise, Roosevelt added more land to our national forests than all preceding presidents, extended the national park system, subsidized a system of state parks, established a new Soil Conservation Service in the Department of Agriculture, and strengthened federal control over western grazing lands. As few other calamities, the Dust Bowl cut to his heart. Conservation, in a dozen agencies, became a gospel. Most visionary and far-reaching, Roosevelt established a national resource planning agency.

The Public Works Administration used a National Planning Board to guide its disparate works program. Under Roosevelt's uncle and veteran city planner, Frederick A. Delano, it was elevated in 1934 to an independent planning agency, the National Resources Committee. Leading American planners and economists—Charles Eliot, Wesley Mitchell, Gardner C. Means—joined Delano. They broadly defined "resources," conducted far-ranging research studies, gave planning advice to many agencies and helped coordinate the work of others, and often recommended unorthodox policy decisions. The committee was independent, learned, visionary, and thus faced intense hostility from Congress, which destroyed it in World War II, but not before it helped set up state and municipal planning agencies throughout the country.

Since recovery remained only a dream in 1933, few home owners and farmers were able to maintain payments on their mortgages (if they had postponed foreclosure for so long). Lending agencies faced great losses, for depreciated property values could not cover many unpaid loans. To aid both financial institutions and home owners, the Home Owners Loan Corporation refinanced mortgages, deferring or spreading out payments and, when necessary, suffering any eventual loss. Thus, banks and lending agencies eventually received full value, while home owners were able to keep their property. At the same time, a newly formed Farm Credit Administration consolidated and extended several loan programs for farmers. The Reconstruction Finance Corporation, a restricted lending agency under Hoover, expanded in all directions, with loans to farmers, small businesses, and even home owners.

Of all early New Deal programs, the Tennessee Valley Authority (TVA) was the most imaginative in conception and one of the most successful in operation. Its roots were mixed, as was its early program. From early progressives came the idea of government-owned utilities and government management of natural resources. Senator George Norris, principal author of the TVA, battled throughout the twenties to implement this policy at Muscle Shoals, Alabama, the site of a wartime nitrate

plant and dam o
advocated limited
regulation and ba
either at conservati
out the twenties, t
group of city plann
Lewis Mumford, ha
the economic and
regions. Arthur S.
had developed a pl
ning while president
owned, relatively au
in World War I l
Corporation. Finall
developed by the A
navigational channe
pork-barrel legislatic

All these ideas
achieved perfect flo
channel, to the lastin
a small town at No
improve rural commu
supported demonstra
In cooperation with
amounted to a secon
of dams and lakes,
areas, while a fores
watersheds. But the
was the production a
choosing dam sites,
planning soon ended.
facile propagandist a
dents of the valley n
planning and looked
corporation. Soon the
lowest cost electricity
use. Cheap electrical

attract industry
raise low living
inevitably takin
some confusion
TVA proved t
possible in gov
New Deal prog
countries.

By the con
New Deal was
effect was overv
his mandate for
Depression and
economic index
the gross nation
Yet almost ever
something to op
one, not even
new agencies. (
relatively major
Democratic ga
ever. He had
endeared himse
sense of confid
roles.

The charm
visibility but h
velt's very fail
greater variety
service. Among
few from the
agencies, news
the glory of the
Eleanor Roose
were dreamers
unconventiona
outlook as he

was unclear about his. They worked on the Consumer Advisory Council of the NRA, carried out research for the National Resources Committee, designed homesteads in Appalachia, or planned minimal budgets for the FERA. A more sophisticated group formed a radical coterie in the AAA and were concerned more for tenant farmers and migratory workers than for the welfare of the Farm Bureau. Others tried to organize miners, felt that Negroes should share equally in New Deal policies, organized community centers and applauded folk art, raved about town meetings, rarely talked for two minutes without mentioning cooperation, and made social concern a mark of acceptability and "conservatism" a mark of Cain. With an assumed air of worldly aplomb, or a carefully cultivated cynicism, many of them tried to hide their idealism and moralism behind their frequent sneers at puritanism, by self-conscious boozing, or, like Harry Hopkins, by conspicuous larks at the races.

These rebels gathered in a hundred corridors to talk and plan and plot their ongoing revolution, their new world a-making. In darker corners, some found their Communist cells and added an apocalyptic urgency to their profound concern. The New Deal went no one place, tried no one thing. But the individual agencies often developed clear plans and tried to achieve them. The New Deal, as a vast and complex whole, denied the idea of experimentation—clear hypotheses and controlled verification. But a dozen agencies were perfect social laboratories and remained so as long as they could hide from the compromises necessitated by politics. These reformers made the New Deal a humane undertaking, in spite of all the callous elements, the conflicting interests, that clashed at the top. Often overly paternalistic, often wonderfully naive, not yet corrupted by any brand of "realism," they worked out the lineaments of a new society, but never came close to achieving it. Instead, they had to quit or learn compromise, many to find a niche in something so mild, so basically cautious, as an embryonic welfare state.

DEPRESSION AMERICA
An Essay in Photographs

I / ON THE FARM

Hell Is Dust

In Colorado in the early thirties

FARM SECURITY ADMINISTRATION-
LIBRARY OF CONGRESS (FSA-LC)

Home Sweet Home   WALKER EVANS, FSA-LC

A Negro cabin in Mississippi (1936)

Lady in White   BEN SHAHN, FSA-LC

Wife of a destitute Ozark tenant farmer (1935)

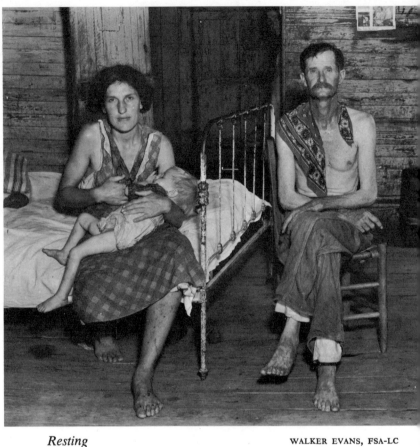

Resting WALKER EVANS, FSA-LC

Alabama sharecropper with wife and child (1935)

Youthful and Hopeful   ARTHUR ROTHSTEIN, FSA-LC

A mountain family, Garrett County, Maryland (1937)

Dignity in Resignation   DOROTHEA LANGE, FSA-LC

An evicted Arkansas sharecropper (1936)

Hoboes, Family Style   DOROTHEA LANGE, FSA-LC

Homeless family of cotton pickers, walking from Phoenix to San Diego (1939)

Rest Stop   DOROTHEA LANGE, FSA-LC

On the way to California, with a sick baby and car trouble

Despair   DOROTHEA LANGE, FSA-LC

**A former Missouri farmer reduced to being a migratory laborer in
California (1936)**

What the Heck? DOROTHEA LANGE, FSA-LC

From Kansas, going west on Route 99

A Home for a Week RUSSELL LEE, FSA-LC

Berry pickers set up housekeeping in a migratory worker's shack, Louisiana (1939)

Hoboes of the Spirit

(Top) An itinerant preacher in a courthouse square, Kentucky

(Bottom) Sidewalk evangelists, Nashville

Heaven   DOROTHEA LANGE, FSA-LC

F.S.A. migratory workers camp, Shafter, California (1938)

Our Daily Bread   EWING GALLOWAY STUDIO

Food line outside a New York City mission

No Work Today

JOHN VACHON, FSA-LC

Unemployed youth, Washington, D.C. (1938)

Just Waiting and Just Sitting

(Top) Unemployed men sunning at San Francisco Public Library (Winter, 1937)

(Bottom) Sit-down strike, Fisher Body Plant (1937)

Black Folks

(Top) Negro homes, Atlanta

(Bottom) Negro family, Washington, D.C.

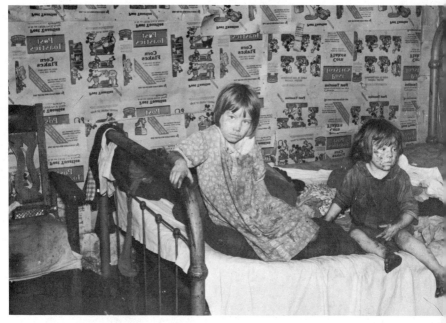

W.P.A. Orphans   MARIAN POST, FSA-LC

Mother has T.B. and father is working for the W.P.A., Charleston, West Virginia (1938)

Happy Days Are Finally Here   JACK DELANO, FSA-LC

**Defense spending brought full-time work for this Georgia textile worker
(1941)**

Dutiful Son   WIDE WORLD

FDR and mother

The Clan

The Roosevelt Family (Christmas 1932)

Inaugural Day   UNITED PRESS INTERNATIONAL

Hoover and FDR (March 4, 1933)

Lion and Mouse   WIDE WORLD

(Top) Hugh Johnson

(Bottom) Harry Hopkins

Braintrusters

(Top) Adolph A. Berle, Jr.

(Bottom) Rexford G. Tugwell

Political Cronies

FDR with Louis Howe (left) and James Farley (right)

Nature Lovers

(Left to right) James Farley, Harold Ickes, R. W. Moore, and FDR at the new Shenandoah National Park

Legislative Triumphs   WIDE WORLD

(Top) Signing T.V.A. legislation (1933)

(Bottom) Approving the Social Security Act (1935)

In Pursuit of Security

WPA-LC

Townsend Headquarters in Vermont (1936)

The W.P.A.   FRANKLIN D. ROOSEVELT LIBRARY

W.P.A. workers clearing up Louisville streets (1937)

The First Job Corps

(Top) FDR at C.C.C. camp in Virginia; flanking him are left to right: Gen. Malone, Howe, Ickes, Fechner, Wallace, and Tugwell

(Bottom) C.C.C. boys planting trees in Montana

T.V.A.

Wilson Dam and nitrate plant, Muscle Shoals, Alabama

Humane Concern   WIDE WORLD

(Top) Harry Hopkins with flood refugees in Arkansas (1937)

(Bottom) Mrs. Roosevelt visiting a work project in Iowa (1936)

THREE

Origins of a Welfare State, 1934–1936

The misery of depression multiplied the need for public welfare. The Democratic sweep in the election of 1934 created a favorable political climate for new federal action. Several New Deal agency heads had already worked out ambitious programs and waited hopefully for funds. Mounting public pressure, often fanned by nostrum-peddling demagogues, helped mute established inhibitions. The Court deathblow to the NRA in 1935, plus congressional pressures, forced Roosevelt to seek a new labor policy, while bitter attacks from a majority of businessmen so angered him that he gladly turned to the working classes for political support. Finally, a growing number of his advisers accepted a monetary, budgetary approach to a still elusive recovery and thus welcomed the deficits involved in large relief programs. These pressures all converged on Congress in 1935, producing a new body of legislation that, with almost unbelievable speed, launched the American welfare state, a brand-new, large, ungainly infant, destined to survive all the hazards of childhood and a maladjusted adolescence, eventually to mature in Lyndon Johnson's Great Society, still ugly but increasingly popular.

The term "welfare state" has many connotations, accompanied by degrees of emotional approval or distaste. To a few Americans it is still an antonym of freedom, a synonym of socialism, a repudiation of responsibility, a catalyst of character decline and civilizational rot. To avowed radicals it connotes halfway, palliative measures, mere sops to the exploited in behalf of preserving privilege and unfair advantage. Rooted in the conservatism of a Bismarck, it is the complete antithesis of a desired socialism. To a much larger group, it is an imperfect but necessary compromise between various contending values and is thus the middle way, the moderate answer. Despite all the bitterness of the thirties, or even of the sixties, a broad spectrum of welfare services has become the norm in America, approved by a substantial majority of the voters. A welfare state is now conventional and orthodox.

In a loose way, everyone favors enhancing the general welfare. The problem is one of means. In the American past the key term was always opportunity, with a type of disciplined freedom closely connected. Governments had a crucial role— protecting and extending opportunity. In this sense, every good state was a welfare state. In a free society, with beckoning opportunities, with no special privileges, each individual or cooperative effort to take advantage of existing opportunities was a lesson in responsibility, an inducement to good character, and a fulfilling experience. Such a simple but profound faith lay at the moralistic heart of American politics. Private property, meaning the actual means of production, and free enterprise, meaning the private right to manage these means, were indispensable elements in this faith. In fact, they were at the heart of a moral society. Everyone should have an opportunity to own and manage, or at least to share in the owning and managing, of productive property. But, to repeat a truism, the faith survived but not the sustaining environment. There was never as much opportunity as the faith presumed. By 1930 only a few people could own and manage property. In this sense opportunity disappeared. But an ersatz type of opportunity—to work for other men, for ever higher wages and ever rising levels of consumption—and an ersatz type of property—common stock, or claims on profits but no real role in management—replaced an earlier dream of farm or shop. In the depression even these poor substitutes paled. Stock values remained so low as to mock past dreams, while up to fifteen million family heads could find no market for their labor and had to turn either to private or to public charity.

This simplified analysis helps clarify the welfare state under Roosevelt and the mixed reception of it. Some welfare measures directed at better opportunity, such as education, had been urged by Jefferson and long since provided by state governments, although Emerson first asked the vital question—opportunity for what, for ownership and enterprise, for responsibility, involvement, and fulfillment, or just opportunity for productive employment? In the New Deal, some legislation, typified by the Farm Tenancy Act of 1937, reflected, realistically or not, the old Jeffersonian idea of true property and true enterprise. Roosevelt eventually launched a devastating attack on entrenched privilege, on monopolistic wealth, on concentrated economic power, on unfair rules in the marketplace. In these emphases, the New Deal was most traditional, not only echoing the language of many self-styled progressives but of an earlier Puritanism. The idea of broad opportunity, the sense of moral responsibility, was an older and deeper orthodoxy than laissez-faire, as such a conventional American, such an able politician, as Roosevelt, always sensed. But much of the welfare legislation of the thirties was of a different sort. Simply, it was a "take-care-of" type of government patronage. The federal government undertook numerous programs to succor the unemployed, the elderly, and the exploited, by direct relief, by work programs, and by regulative laws that forced employers to be more generous.

Penetrating criticisms of government charity came from both sides of the political spectrum. To Herbert Hoover, the assumption of direct responsibility for the individual by any government, and particularly by a distant federal government, endangered the whole idea of personal integrity and misconstrued the area of responsibility rightly reserved for government. Sustained gifts from governments would create a passive, alienated group of men, without a real stake in society, with no compelling involvement, and with a dangerous political tendency to march in step with any demagogue promising more welfare. He always insisted that the long-range welfare of the individual could only be served by his active, creative participation in our private economy, and not by accepting some dole, concealed or not. Thus welfare was a dangerous answer to depression; recovery and restored opportunity the only legitimate, long-term answer.

Hoover did not fulfill the logic of his position, for he tried somehow to salvage the ideal of individual opportunity in the midst of large, centralized corporations. At Vanderbilt University, a group of literary critics, who called themselves Fugitives or Southern Agrarians, argued that large, collective enterprise precluded individual freedom and opportunity. They advocated a return to Jefferson's America, to a truly propertied society. They wanted to break up large, impersonal economic units, decentralize economic decision making, and redistribute the means of production to each family. They deplored large corporations and large factories, massed in ugly and inhumane cities, with a few capitalists making all important decisions, with most workers concerned only with extrinsic returns and with the consumption of standardized and ugly products. Such a system left most people servile, dependent on paternalistic masters. To turn captains of industry into government bureaucrats, to substitute government collectivism for private, would do little to cure the ills of the existing society. Likewise, paternal welfare measures could only increase the servility and alienating effects of an already oppressive society.

On the socialist left, the most astute critics also decried the new welfare state. But, unlike Hoover they did not expect to solve the problems of depression by restoring the business society of the twenties. Unlike the agrarians, they saw no realistic prospect of returning to real property and individual entrepreneurship. They felt that welfare measures obscured the continued injustices of corporate capitalism, thus allaying rightful demands for economic justice. Welfare, by stilling the voice of dissent, and by stimulating more consumption and higher profits, represented a type of government insurance for the existing economy. Even a slight leveling of wealth or even truly progressive taxes would not restore true opportunity. Instead of aid to the unemployed, the existing economic system had to be replaced by one that not only guaranteed employment but that gave to all citizens, even in large-scale production, some sense of personal involvement and some share in ownership and management. These socialists, whether Christians, Marxists, or pragmatists, still had the old vision of a cooperative commonwealth.

But the battle over welfare legislation, then or now, usually did not revolve around fundamental issues. On one level the advocacy or opposition was framed in light of immediate economic interest. This included both those who asked, "What can I get?" as well as those who cried, "What will it cost me?" The battle of interests was clothed in the folklore of our society, in the myths accepted by millions of people. Thus many wrapped the verbal icons of Jefferson tightly around the most unpalatable injustices and the most transparent privileges. Or they used old clichés from the populist and progressive eras, now stripped of their real meanings, to oversimplify the very complexities that demanded thought and laborious action.

The welfare legislation of 1935, and the political rationale that accompanied it, occasioned critical divergence among Roosevelt's staff and also among later historians. Raymond

Moley first condemned Roosevelt for deserting a true concert of interests and for discontinuing early cooperative overtures to business. To him, the new welfare measures, joined with the class appeals in the campaign of 1936, represented a demagogic radicalism and a betrayal of all Roosevelt's early promises. In a loose way, most historians, including textbook authors, accepted Moley's contention that Roosevelt moved to the "left" in 1935. Reflecting their own political preferences, most approved the shift. Tugwell demurred, as did contemporary socialist critics. He agreed with Moley that Roosevelt had donned progressive icons, probably for political reasons rather than as a legitimate turn to the left. He saw it as a "conservative" betrayal of the concert of interests, which he defined as planning rather than Moley's partnership with business. For Tugwell, the old, divisive class rhetoric, however radical it sounded, was only a political smoke screen employed to disguise the return of America to private manipulators.

The largest welfare program of the New Deal, and of American history, began in 1935. A newly elected, exceedingly generous Congress approved a $4,880,000,000 Emergency Relief Appropriation, to be spent as Roosevelt saw fit. This was, up until this time, the largest appropriation in American history and the largest accretion to the national debt. Roosevelt used it to consolidate and expand numerous early, temporary relief programs, which had served up to thirty million people. About $1,500,000,000, the largest single block, went to Harry Hopkins and to a new relief organization created by executive order, the huge Works Progress Administration (WPA). In turn, the WPA used most of its share, plus endless new appropriations, for work programs for the unemployed. At times its projects resembled those of the more reputable PWA, even as a favored Hopkins cut into what Ickes believed should have been his share of the appropriation. Against the wishes of organized labor, WPA wage rates were below those of private industry; anyone offered private employment became ineligible for WPA work. Burdened by a lack of developed plans for massive public works, by an oversupply of unskilled laborers, and by rigid rules, the WPA was inefficient by any private standard. Nonetheless, the completed projects in part compensated for the money spent and represented a great gain over direct doles. Despite vigorous efforts to maintain high morale, and despite the sincere appreciation of most workers, the WPA could not escape some of the stigma of relief. In fact, derisive opponents would not let it. Also, the WPA could only employ about a third of those who needed work, leaving millions to the care or neglect of states. Many had to remain on a dole, often supplemented by free food distributed by a Federal Surplus Commodities Corporation.

Less expensive and more daring were the several white collar programs set up by the WPA, drawing upon earlier experiences of the CWA and some State Relief Administrations. For the first time in American history, the federal government gave a vast subsidy to some of the fine arts and to scholarship (Federal Theater, Federal Writers', and Federal Art projects). Much of the art, particularly plays, sculpture, and painting, reflected the social concern of the thirties. The most rewarding aspect of these programs was the degree of participation. Music, painting, and the theater, usually frivolous sideshows of the wealthy, centered in a few large cities and priced beyond the common people, now merged with daily life, in murals on public buildings, in local symphonies, in amateur theaters. Just as important, thousands of people were able to participate in creative endeavors, including handicrafts. Another subagency, the National Youth Administration, directed by Hopkins's assistant, Aubrey Williams, inaugurated a vast scholarship program under the guise of student work, and set up work projects for school dropouts.

A second large block of the relief appropriation went to Rexford G. Tugwell, who headed another new agency, the Resettlement Administration (RA). It absorbed the rural relief and rehabilitation programs of the old FERA and the uncompleted communities of the Division of Subsistence Homesteads. Tugwell had more plans than funds. As the title suggests, he wanted to resettle urban slum dwellers in autonomous garden cities and submarginal farmers in new, productive farm villages, with cooperation a guiding concern of both groups. His greatest monuments were three suburban greenbelt cities and a few dozen new farm communities. The largest share of his funds had to be used to continue a rural relief program. Disillusioned by the failure of the AAA to become an instrument of rural reform, and long contemptuous of the Extension Service, Tugwell set up a duplicate farm organization, with its own agents, but dedicated only to the exploited and underprivileged.

The RA would not compromise with existing evils. Almost alone, it fought for equal benefits for Negroes. It was the only New Deal agency to set up group medical plans. Contrary to the idols of Congress and to the ruling commitment of the Department of Agriculture, RA leaders questioned fee simple ownership and experimented both with long-term leases and with cooperative farms. Concerned with farm labor, it set up migratory camps and tried to alleviate the plight of the "Okies." But in most cases it loaned funds to small farmers for needed equipment or vital necessities and then supervised their farm program, protected them from exploitation, and took a percentage of their crops as repayment. The RA became a new, solicitous bank for small landowners and a second, protective landlord for tenants. It was not only one of the most honest but probably the most class-conscious of New Deal agencies. Soon it antagonized practically every vested interest, a good mark of its relative effectiveness. Yet its funds permitted it only to touch the problems of rural areas, particularly in the South. With restricted prerogatives, plus a tenant-purchase program at odds with its earlier orientation, the RA moved into the Department of Agriculture in 1937 and became the Farm Security Administration (FSA). Congress gleefully destroyed it during the war, replacing it with an attenuated Farmers' Home Administration.

The Social Security Act of 1935 became the supreme symbol of a welfare state. As enacted, it hardly deserved the honor or opprobrium. But it set enduring precedents and established a new area of federal responsibility. The bill was tremendously complex, compromising many divergent plans and establishing an array of welfare programs. Although not responsible for the details of the act, Roosevelt had worked for better old-age benefits and for unemployment insurance while governor of New York. As early as 1934 he signed a Railroad Retirement Act. In the same year, he witnessed the growing frustration of the underprivileged classes, who had so far reaped a bitter harvest in New Deal recovery programs. With unfulfilled expectations, revolutionary feelings grew even faster than in 1932. Various movements, often roughly but arbitrarily classed to the right and left, gained vast public support. Two of these, led by Huey Long and Francis E. Townsend, focused on the extremes of wealth in America and proffered schemes for either sharing the wealth (Long) or providing elaborate pensions for the elderly (Townsend). Naive or oversimplified, their platforms revivified the old problem of Henry George—great wealth and great poverty. Roosevelt, as a good politician, saw the tremendous political appeal of legislation directed at the elderly and unemployed and thus joined his support to that of congressional authors. Even most Republicans, with apprehensive glances over their left shoulders and aware of the mildness of the final version, supported the bill.

The Social Security Act set up the present compulsory tax for retirement benefits, a tax assessed in equal parts on employer and employee. The original act excluded about half the people, including farmers, domestics, and the elderly. The employee tax represented a significant drain from already low payrolls and thus a further obstacle to recovery. The original act did not protect against accidents and illness before retirement, provided no medical insurance, and paid benefits on the basis of past earning instead of present need. Thus it was close to a compulsory insurance system, paid for largely by those who benefited. The unemployment insurance provision delegated most responsibility to the states and invited chaotic variations in always inadequate payments. Since the retirement coverage was so limited, the act provided matching federal funds for traditional state pensions for the aged and funds for dependent mothers, children, and the crippled and blind. These supplemental programs now provide the most crucial support for our present, locally administered public welfare system, with all its confusions and endlessly criticized inadequacies.

In housing, as in retirement, the New Deal made modest, even parsimonious, but precedent-breaking commitments. Continuing a program begun under Hoover, the PWA loaned funds to local, limited-dividend housing corporations, for both housing projects and slum clearance. Under Ickes's watchful eyes, the PWA approved only a few projects (less than 25,000 housing units completed by 1937). The several community programs involved only limited numbers but, in the case of the greenbelt towns of the Resettlement Administration, quite imaginative but uncopied experiments, not only in housing but in community planning. Beginning in 1934 the government tried to stimulate private construction, aid home buyers, and protect mortgage bankers through a loan insurance program administered by a new Federal Housing Administration (FHA). Since the FHA assumed final responsibility for repayment (a service paid for by a tax on borrowers) and required certain standards in construction, this program helped many middle-income families buy homes at a low rate of interest. In the thirties the FHA did not appreciably stimulate private home building and thus failed as a recovery measure, but it became the financial backbone of a boom in private home construction after World War II. Finally, in 1937, after years of effort by housing and urban renewal proponents, and particularly by Senator Robert F. Wagner of New York, Roosevelt agreed to support a subsidized housing and slum-clearance program. The Wagner-Steagall Act established the United States Housing Authority as a government corporation. It had $500,000,000 to loan to state or local housing authorities. The terms were generous, with low interest and extended (sixty years) repayments. When housing projects replaced slums, annual contributions by the USHA further subsidized the program. Federal rules required rents well below competitive rates and limited residency to low-income families. The first results, under local direction, were almost universally ugly and depressing developments, segregated, stigmatized by their origin and by residency requirements, resented by local citizens, and located in the worst sections of town.

Relief, unemployment insurance, and low-income housing all represented tangible, if limited, benefits for working people and the unemployed. Roosevelt wanted to help farmers and laborers gain minimal economic security as part of their American birthright. He did not easily move beyond this commitment. Paternal business, if paternal enough, seemed adequate. Early in his presidency, he easily cooperated with businessmen who shared his humane concern and in several cases sided with business in labor-management disputes. Thus, until 1935, he was clearly proagriculture, even prolabor, but not prounion. But events pushed him into the camp of the labor unions. Section 7 (a) of the NIRA, if liberally interpreted, was indeed the long-awaited Magna Carta of organized labor. In part frustrated by company unions, never given adequate protection by the NRA staff, the American Federation of Labor nonetheless acted as if it were a Magna Carta and began large organizational drives. In 1934, strikes erupted throughout the country, often directed by labor radicals rather than by the cautious AFL. From the impetus of the strikes came the revolutionary rise of industrial unions, the schism of 1935, and the vitality and political effectiveness of the new Congress of Industrial Organizations. Militant unionism had its golden age in the thirties. Dramatic sit-down strikes only highlighted a successful union struggle for recognition by most large national corporations. As a whole, union workers loved and supported Roosevelt, while business leaders reviled him. With the death of NRA, Roosevelt had to choose a new labor policy. He belatedly chose the side of the unions. They had votes and loved a Roosevelt willing to show some interest in their problems.

If 7 (a) was the Magna Carta, the National Labor Relations Act of 1935 (Wagner Act) was the Bill of Rights for unions. It involved an almost unbelievable capitulation by the government. The architect of the bill, Senator Wagner, served as chairman of the National Labor Board under the NRA.

Frustrated by the business-oriented leadership of Hugh Johnson, the board had limited success in protecting workers. In 1934 Roosevelt established a National Labor Relations Board (NLRB) as a separate, but rather futile, agency which still had to utilize the statutory provisions of the NIRA. As a result, Wagner fought, without Roosevelt's blessing, for new statutory authority and a new, more powerful NLRB. His bill passed the Senate in 1935 without administration support, and then with it breezed through the House. The bill guaranteed the right of collective bargaining by a union chosen by a majority of employees, legalized collective action (strikes, boycotts), and by a code of fair practices outlawed such traditional weapons as the company union, blacklist, and yellow-dog contract. The act empowered a new NLRB to conduct representation elections and hear any complaints from unions. Big labor, in one sweep, almost gained equality with big business. But for the majority of workers, as yet unorganized, the Wagner Act was less important than Social Security. Tied to the interstate commerce clause, it did not protect the bargaining rights of public employees, service and agricultural workers, and workers in strictly intrastate commerce.

The welfare legislation, large in hopes generated, often small in actual benefits, hardly represented a social revolution. Except for relief, only a small burden had been added to the national budget, and none of the welfare programs significantly redistributed the wealth of the country. Not only Huey Long, but politicians of varied persuasions wanted to lessen disparities of income and accumulated wealth. Some Congressmen, influenced by Louis Brandeis and like foes of centralized power, also wanted to help restore competition by placing a tax on bigness. Roosevelt, enraged by hostile newspapers and by business criticism, increasingly advised by Felix Frankfurter (then at the Harvard Law School and a Brandeis disciple), and always thirsting for a good fight, presented Congress with a new and biting tax proposal in the spring of 1935. It had two purposes: a fairer sharing of the tax burden and penalties on large enterprise. The bill, soon labeled a "soak-the-rich" measure, provoked an embittered controversy. It marked the most decisive turn by Roosevelt from consensus politics to a clear appeal to the disinherited. The tax message rested on the depressing fact that, so far, New Deal policies had created a more regressive tax system, with greater burdens on consumption and low incomes than on large incomes. Large corporations had used the depression to reduce debts and to increase their liquid capital, even while suffering operating losses, suspending dividends, and thus avoiding taxes. Also, then as now, large incomes escaped existing tax schedules by loopholes and avoidance.

Roosevelt asked for a graduated corporate income tax, a separate intercorporate dividend tax to prevent an escape via subsidiary companies, an inheritance and gift tax, and a more sharply graduated income tax. His message to Congress was loaded with encomiums for small enterprise and diatribes against business concentration and large accumulations of wealth. In Congress, Roosevelt, who never pushed the tax bill as strenuously as other legislation, suffered a mild defeat. Congress passed only a token corporate income tax. It dropped the inheritance tax. In all, small tax increases produced only $250,000,000 in annual revenue. The bill neither soaked the rich, penalized bigness, nor significantly helped balance the budget. A later (1936) tax on undistributed dividends and excess profits was likewise attenuated and subsequently repealed. Thus tax policy was not to play an important role in New Deal economic policy, at least beyond the realm of rhetoric and psychological warfare.

But the battle against bigness became a standard New Deal brand. Not that it ever achieved significant results. That was almost impossible. The emphasis shifted only after the demise of the NRA. In crucial industries like coal, petroleum, and the retail trades, with many small producers, the federal government almost of necessity continued an NRA type of detailed regulation and protection under new, more carefully drafted legislation. In industries dominated by a few large producers, the collusion and accommodation once again became a private, in part clandestine operation, while Roosevelt's avowed policy was free competition, the prosecution of monopoly, and concessions to small business. Under Thurman Arnold, beginning in 1938, the Antitrust Division of the Department of Justice expanded its operations to the highest level in history, perhaps as much for punitive reasons as for restored competition or, as even Arnold suggested, as a type of folk ritual that at least pointed to the ultimate superiority of government over the corporations.

The most vulnerable area of chaotic and wasteful bigness was in the electrical utilities, where pyramiding holding companies often controlled the companies that produced and distributed power. In the wake of the TVA battles, here were identified political devils. With some glee, Roosevelt asked Congress to pass a Public Utilities Holding Company Act, which would empower the SEC to simplify and rationalize the holding companies to make geographic and economic sense and to abolish those without economic justification (the "death sentence"). It also authorized the Federal Power Commission to integrate, under federal controls, operating companies into regional systems. All hell broke loose. Led by able apologists such as Wendell Willkie, and by less ethical lobbyists by the hundreds, the utility companies spent a billion dollars to defeat or emasculate the bill. As its first direct slap at Roosevelt, Congress amended the death sentence amid turbulent accusations of unfair lobbying and unfair administration pressure, both true.

The private utilities won a minor skirmish, not a war. They still faced severe regulation. Also, in line with TVA, the administration added vast public power projects at Grand Coulee and Hoover dams and tried for years to get additional valley authorities. In 1935, under the Emergency Relief Appropriation, Roosevelt set up a Rural Electrification Administration (REA), which could not construct rural power facilities but which used low-interest loans in an unsuccessful attempt to encourage private companies to serve rural areas. In 1936 Congress made the REA into an independent lending agency, against a last, vengeful outpouring of vituperation from private

promote consumer buying in periods of mild recession. But in such deep depressions as that of the thirties, central banking policies are almost useless unless supported by budgetary and tax measures or by direct controls. There simply was no demand for easy credit. Absurdly low interest rates could not induce enough buying or investment for recovery. The new Federal Reserve controls, added to the sustained incomes provided by Social Security, were good tools for fighting against another severe depression but impotent for recovery. Eccles realized this and advocated continued deficit spending, preferably on large public works projects. He lectured fellow bankers on the archaic and misinformed idea that anything but small, balanced governmental budgets would lead to inflation and eventual economic collapse. In the thirties, surplus production and low demand precluded inflation. Except for managed prices under the early NRA and AAA, no serious price inflation occurred in the thirties, apart from a brief, artificial spurt just before the recession of 1937. It came at the one time when government budgets were in balance.

Beginning in 1935, and parallel with massive relief expenditures, almost all economic indexes moved upward. The valley of depression slowly gave way to the foothills of recovery, a recovery too often defined as a return to 1929 levels, as if continued growth were unthinkable. The weaknesses were obvious. Unemployment, after declining from the peak of 1933 (twelve to fifteen million), sank to approximately eight million and stuck there. Consumer buying remained well below 1929. The construction industries remained pitifully depressed at only one-fourth the high level of the twenties. The economy had achieved only an equilibrium of slow growth. Yet the old idea of a mature economy persisted. Many New Dealers, including Roosevelt, were happy with the rising charts. In the campaign of 1936 he promised to battle against the remaining ills of the economy and against the selfish men who prevented full victory, and proudly took credit for having lifted America from depression.

By 1936 the depression should have been over. "Ifs"

abound. If businessmen in particular had understood New Deal policies and had responded in confidence rather than unreasonable fear. If Roosevelt had not, by 1936, turned in devastating fury upon business and thus fanned resentment and increased confusion. If Roosevelt, rather than using business leaders as scapegoats and merely badgering the corporations with diversionary but essentially harmless policies, had really turned toward increased federal direction and ownership. Or if the government, in spite of early promises of economy, had pumped such enormous sums of borrowed money into the economy that it had to respond.

The last strategy was the going fad among intellectuals. Keynes had just published his epochal *General Theory of Employment, Interest and Money*, in which he plotted in mathematical exactitude the multiplying effects of central banking, tax, and budgetary policies on a market economy. But even large government investments were only stimulants. They could be resisted by countervailing factors that inhibited private spending. It seemed that between 1933 and 1937 the New Deal floundered between ever more daring banking and budgetary measures on one hand and ever more uncertain and stubborn business leaders on the other. Every new economic stimulant acted as a depressant on the minds of the affluent. This was aggravated by the almost total lack of dialogue between the government and business.

By 1936 the New Deal was submerged in irony. To understand this is to get at the heart of the history of the thirties and to get a much better perspective on the welfare state. At the national level, Roosevelt emerged in the clothing of a great progressive reformer. From his early attempts to understand the economic issues, from the tutelage of the brain trust, or even of the gold faddists, he moved to a firm posture—against bigness, against unearned privileges, against economic selfishness; and for the little man, for the exploited, for good and unselfish people everywhere. To Raymond Moley, this class appeal represented a damaging radicalism. To Tugwell, it represented a political sideshow, for it concealed a turn to a very traditional economic philosophy, and with it a permanent rejection of real planning.

Both were correct. Roosevelt did move away from economic realities and into the lair of the demagogue. Of course most leaders of large business were selfish. But small businessmen were also selfish and by all odds more so than large ones. So were labor leaders, and, believe it or not, even farmers. The charge was meaningless. Of course many selfish and short-sighted businessmen, particularly small businessmen, did what they could without punishment in the pursuit of profits, even in some cases where the law forbade. So do most men. They even did it with full assurance that it was right, that the whole country gained from their daring enterprise. Not only did they do it, they would continue to do it, unless stripped of the power to do it or converted to a whole new world view that prevented it (an unlikely answer in spite of Roosevelt's sermons). But Roosevelt kept preaching his denunciatory sermons. He fanned the resentment of good, as well as of selfish and jealous, Americans without power and of farsighted or politically loyal ones with power. He stimulated righteous indignation and the atmosphere of a moral crusade. But the crusade could do nothing except take punitive action: divide a holding company, threaten but never collect progressive taxes, or use welfare measures to uplift the downtrodden victims of evil men.

The crusade almost always ended in some degree of futility. The battle for the "people" had to eventuate in legislation, had to pass through Roosevelt and the Congress, and then stand up in the courts. In Roosevelt's terms, every New Deal "reform" was a generous act by good men of power against bad men of power. In fact, it was usually a confused compromise by an indistinguishable mixture of good and bad men of power, with Roosevelt (abetted by many historians) generally finding most Republican politicians, recalcitrant Southern Democrats, and at least four Supreme Court judges to be bad men of power, allied to numerous bad men throughout the country. But neither bad men nor good men saw much beyond the evident selfishness of their opponents. Thus, instead of recognizing real devils, or contemplating major but almost impossible changes in American institutions or in the real power structure (not the party structure), the good men either tried some mild detergent in futile efforts to clean up the existing system or tried to appease and care for those who were suffering because of its inadequacies.

The good men of power were as much a part of the system as the bad men of power. They could not see that monopoly was a natural and not necessarily harmful end result of a private market system, that negative regulation in behalf of competition would not, could not, and possibly should not work, and that more biting, more stringent positive controls would be truly revolutionary, that is, would force a shift of economic and political control, and thus often threaten their own privileged positions. Even when Roosevelt, conventional in beliefs but pleasingly archaic in his gentlemanly noblesse oblige, or his academic advisers (presumably good men without power) framed legislation that had some bite, such as a pure food and drugs act or a tax reform bill, it rarely survived Congress. When an ambiguous, potentially radical program did survive, or was sneaked in by executive order, it was usually neutralized by administrators, nullified by the courts, endlessly frustrated in its day-to-day operations, or eventually destroyed or emasculated for political reasons.

The story of most New Deal frustration remains untold. The thirties were indeed a time of reform, a period when sensitivity to injustice, to vast structures of privilege, to the terribly empty lives of most people, prevailed as never before. Much of the concern remained outside government, in critics of the New Deal, in radical political movements, in artists of varied mediums, in a few philosophers. But many reformers worked in or with New Deal agencies, particularly the relief agencies. They were always in the minority and had to fight an unending battle within their own agencies. But the outside battle was the main one. As they struggled to carry out their programs, dealing directly with the exploited people who loved Roosevelt, they often found their task impossible. The economic and social institutions of a Democratic South, as an example, presented one tremendous source of frustration. Blocked at every turn, they learned anew the ever relevant lesson of Lincoln Steffens. Those who effectively frustrated their efforts also loved Roosevelt and were on the side of the angels. They were also powerful. The devils could be dealt with, but not the angels. Mrs. Roosevelt knew their plight, and they loved her for knowing. On occasion, F.D.R. knew also and, when political realities permitted, tried to help his loyal good men without power. But nothing in his leadership was capable of transforming the desires of these loyal reformers into a new structure of political power. It may have been impossible, even had he tried. Master of politics, he was also captive to politics. Thus the story of many New Deal agencies was a sad story, the ever recurring story of what might have been. Perhaps only Tugwell showed a full appreciation of this sadness, but even he quickly returned to the charisma of an adored leader.

Since the New Deal failed to fulfill even the minimal dream of most of the varied reformers, why did all the "evil" men of power, plus millions of Republican dupes, oppose it? To Roosevelt, the answer was simple: they were evil. Economic royalists, with a monopoly of power, they were not content with a repaired and honest capitalism. Instead, they wanted to drive on with their plutocracy and bring down upon the heads of the good men of power the inevitable revolution. Then good bankers would suffer and good businessmen might lose the management of their corporations. But this answer, although in part true, was too simple. The opponents of Roosevelt misconstrued the direction of the New Deal. Many believed Roosevelt's class language. They really thought America was losing its "free" capitalist soul to some type of socialism. In their praise of freedom lurked some valuable and perceptive criticism of the New Deal and of an ever more powerful federal government. Also, many Americans, perhaps particularly the monied classes, never trusted Roosevelt, much less some of his advisers. The New Deal was indeed a mixed company, a type of political bohemia, frequented by many of the better sort, but still dangerous. Roosevelt was a puzzling creature. Even when he abetted existing privileges, he preached an alien gospel. Let us have anything but a righteous gentleman in Washington. Even a Marxist would have made more sense to them. Finally, almost no one expected vast economic expansion, and thus no one could see welfare as other than a permanent liability, somehow drawn from the ledger of profits or high incomes, either directly by taxes or indirectly by government deficits and inflation. The threat to earnings, the inhibition to investment, seemed the central issue, more important than declining fears of revolution, humane concern, or an occasional recognition of the importance of purchasing power.

But the supreme irony is here. The enemies of the New Deal were wrong. They should have been friends. Security was a prime concern of the insecure thirties. It cut across all classes. Businessmen, by their policies, desperately sought it in lowered corporate debts and tried to get the government to practice the same austerity. Even when ragged and ill-housed, workers opened savings accounts. The New Deal, by its policies, underwrote a vast apparatus of security. But the meager benefits of Social Security were insignificant in comparison to the building system of security for large, established business. But like stingy laborers, the frightened businessmen did not use and enjoy this security and thus increase it. The New Deal tried to frame institutions to protect the economy from major business cycles and began in an unclear sort of way to underwrite continuous economic growth and sustained profits. Although some tax bills at least hinted at restrictions on high profits, the New Deal certainly never attacked profits. During the thirties taxes did not contribute to any leveling of income. If one counts Social Security deductions and such indirect levies as the processing taxes by the AAA, New Deal taxation was regressive. Because of tax policies, even relief expenditures became disguised subsidies to producers, since future taxes on individual salaries or on consumer goods would pay for most relief. Thus, instead of higher wages creating a market, at the short-term expense of profits, the government supported market demand without taking the cost out of the hides of businessmen as they expected and feared.

Even at the local level there would be no significant shift in the economic and social structure, despite the idealistic goals of agency officials. Negroes, politically purchased by relief or by the occasional concern of bureaucrats or Mrs. Roosevelt, remained a submerged and neglected caste. Service and farm labor, including migratory, received slight succor. Millions continued in desultory enslavement to immediate needs. Thus the people of greatest economic power gained added security and lost only undisciplined freedom and a degree of popular respect. The last they regained quickly. Most of all, the individual farmer lost some entrepreneurial freedom and accepted a degree of central planning, although through democratic procedures. Even manufacturing industries had to accept new procedural limitations—labor laws, added regulatory agencies, new taxes, and minimum wage and maximum hours. But these contributed to security and to ordered growth. Even without government action, many such restraints were already part of large corporations, as early as the twenties. Security demanded procedural rules, a degree of uniformity, and even a formalized relationship with organized labor. Only small, aggressive adventurers or promoters suffered from the new procedural limitations. The only leveling, and the only real bite, hit certain middle-income groups and some small businesses. Perhaps the Chambers of Commerce were correct in condemning Roosevelt in 1935. The National Association of Manufacturers was not.

Government spending in behalf of multiplied private spending, the strongest weapon of Eccles and Keynes, was to be the final and most complete insurance policy for the existing American economy. After 1937, even Roosevelt reluctantly swallowed this pill. Keynes was the last great classical economist, in the tradition of Adam Smith, Ricardo, the Mills, Marx, and Marshall. A British Liberal, formal, analytical, he tried to devise the minimal government devices necessary to maintain most of the free aspects of a market system. At the beginning of this greatest economic tradition, Adam Smith tried to get the freedom. At the end, Keynes tried to keep as much as possible. He wanted to set up safeguards to prevent serious depressions, to maintain full employment, and at the same time to provide all the welfare measures required by humane concern. He wanted to avoid socialist ownership and bureaucratic management on one hand and the severe controls of a corporate state on the other. His complex arguments had small influence on the New Deal, but his general prescription eventually prevailed.

The magic in Keynes, at least for an interval, was the magic of growth itself, which springs from new knowledge but is implemented through political economy. Growth can raise a whole society, with rising profits matching rising wages and rising government income supporting rising welfare measures. Business, so fearful of new welfare, never realized that it could be paid for by government credit and that public debts could be maintained (or repaid) without extra tax rates and without a significant redistribution of income or wealth. Roosevelt wanted some redistribution. Like Keynes, he had social as well as economic goals. But he rarely achieved these—witness again the congressional compromises and the frustrated bureaucrats on the moral battlefield. During World War II, when massive spending purchased unbelievable growth, Roosevelt had to suspend social goals and let the public subsidize plant expansion, profits, and, above all, future profits. By then he had no political alternative. Full employment, plus overtime, reduced the welfare burden, while growth and temporarily high taxes helped pay the cost of war. With full employment, some temporary leveling finally occurred. After the war the large government subsidy to business continued—in huge defense purchases, in contracts awarded in behalf of corporate survival, in research, in tax relief, in a flexible use of antitrust laws, in enough welfare increases to soothe the discontented, in a tacit acceptance of administered prices, and increasingly even in an unwillingness to antagonize the business community (even Democrats learned the old Hoover bit about confidence).

The battle between economic leaders and the New Deal

was never complete. Some businessmen and many large farmers (historians generally call them enlightened) supported Roosevelt throughout the thirties. Many more, if they had understood Roosevelt's purposes, would surely have backed him. In the same sense, Roosevelt, considering his objectives, his willingness to retain and strengthen a private economy, should have worked more at understanding and communicating with businessmen, for their choices had more to do with the success of the New Deal than anything else. Yet, a real issue divided the two. Simply, it was a matter of power. Roosevelt was powerful and could not be controlled by anyone or by any group. In this sense he was incorruptible, perhaps as much so as any president in American history. For two years even intense lobbying could not block his sway over the legislative process. Tugwell always believed his leadership offered the potential for a major shift in government. Had Roosevelt responded to academic advisers, he could have effected policies which seriously invaded the prerogatives of major private interests. Instead of a limited socialization of product via welfare, Tugwell believed Roosevelt could have socialized management or even the plant. He never did this; seemingly, he never wanted to, but until 1937 he seemed to have the political power and never gave enough assurances to convince businessmen that he might not. For a while, he circumvented their normal channels of power to the federal government. This is why they had to turn over and over again to the federal courts as their last desperate refuge. But even as Roosevelt secured great political power, and thus potential economic power, the power of economic decision making remained perilously in private hands, less secure and less potent than ever before. The tense situation could not endure.

The shift to welfare policies and then to Keynesian recovery policies took away most of the threat and left private corporate interests shaken but more secure than ever. Nationalization and economic planning, which never had extensive popular support, were dead issues after 1935. The government would now use banking and budgetary policies to protect, support, and occasionally discipline private producers. This meant a helping hand for private industry, but with too many obligations, too many secure guarantees, and too many restrictions for many old-fashioned industrialists. Security does reduce freedom.

But the government had, more clearly than ever in the past, committed itself to national economic goals. This was one of the enduring consequences of the New Deal. Since the federal government rejected planning (except to a degree in agriculture) and refused to do its own producing, it had no alternative but to rely on the major corporations and to subsidize them if necessary to insure its goals of rapid growth, high levels of employment, and low welfare needs. Even a slight increase in private economic activity can do more to benefit the country than vast welfare programs. Precluded from direct economic action, the government had to use indirect controls and incentives, plus persuasion, bribes, or, if politically possible, threats and punitive measures. In this situation, high profits rightfully became desirable public policy, since they usually increased the total economic activity and the level of national prosperity. In spite of all the ridicule, nothing was now truer than the quip: "What is good for General Motors is good for the country." Under the emerging system, the welfare of both were inseparable.

The dependence was mutual. The large corporations, protected by a generous government against the insecurity of the past (when politicians could safely allow depressions) and also against their own worst mistakes and abuses, were tied to government policies. The national budget was almost as important as their corporate budgets. The action of the Federal Reserve Board, or even random pronouncements by government officials, could wreck their best laid plans. Welfare spending became a vital part of the total market for goods, forcing some business acquiescence even here. In a few areas, such as low-rent housing, welfare programs became the major support for very profitable businesses. Later, defense spending would completely support large companies and provide the margin of profit for hundreds. Increasingly, business and government were linked in more subtle ways, particularly by a common economic orthodoxy and a common need for certain skills. Bureaucrats moved from Ivy League campuses to corporations and on to Washington. The situation invited, in fact necessitated, cooperation, or a truly joint enterprise. Roosevelt cleared the way for such cooperation, but he never desired it or achieved it and probably never perceived its inescapable logic. Unlike most politicians, he was never a good businessman, nor could he share power easily. The old, individualistic capitalist did not fit the new picture. Mavericks were taboo. But neither did reformers fit. The new partnership, with greater government participation and greater benefits (the welfare state for business), left room for tension, even bitter conflict, as between mutually dependent husband and wife. Always, one or the other partner could try to gain too much power and upset the partnership. Each appealed to an overlapping but never identical constituency. Generally, with time and enough advice from Keynesian counselors, the two settled into almost blissful matrimony. What about the constituency? For business, shareholders have profited. Dividends have been large and capital accumulation even larger. The larger constituency of government presents a much more variegated pattern. But most able and fortunate people, if they have been loyal, have received well in material returns and have profited from the general benevolence and good will of both the private and government bureaucrats who look out for them.

But the economic magic of sustained growth and the political magic of welfare can be irrelevant to moral and religious vision, which may also demand a just community. For the more sensitive New Dealers, or outside critics, Keynes provided a technique for priming the economic pump but no means of purifying the water. They thirsted after the pure product. Growth could simply intoxicate the affluent minority (or majority), blunt their sensitivity, and leave them in satiated lethargy, full but unfulfilled. Welfare could do the same for the poor. Growth could lead to vast production, to an enormous gross national product, but also to ugliness and spiritual poverty everywhere. It might even lead to full employment and undreamed-of security (goals never fully attained), yet to a society bereft of meaningful work, of personal involvement, even of democratic participation. It might suggest the blessing of leisure but bring only the curse of idleness. Finally, it would surely conceal injustice and leave the exploited to the tender and prejudiced mercy of local conscience. During the war the disturbing reformers dropped from view and did not emerge again until the sixties. Then, to the profound surprise of all good men of power, the one-third ill-fed and ill-housed, and the two-thirds alienated and desperate, still existed. In spite of the New Deal and in spite of all that welfare!

*

FOUR

The Perils of
Depression Politics,
1936–1938

The legislative climax of 1935 preceded the political climax of
the New Deal in 1936. But again, as in 1932, Roosevelt won no
mandate for specific new programs. Then, in the Court fight and
the new depression, both in 1937, he lost much of his political
leverage. By 1938 he was frustrated in his domestic policies and
imprisoned by neutrality legislation in his early ventures into
international diplomacy. After a desperate attempt at party

realignment, he began buying congressional help in foreign policy at the expense of further domestic innovation. The New Deal was over.

Roosevelt won the election in 1935. By giving the Democratic party prior claims to the welfare state, he established it as the party of generous concern, committed to a government for the people. He personally symbolized the concern. His programs, however limited, and his promises, however vague, supported the symbol. In 1936 a slow recovery increased its tempo. Carefully, Roosevelt continued the relief programs at full strength. In Congress he trod lightly, asking only for an undistributed profits tax to help balance the budget. His opponents, both Republicans and disillusioned Democrats, were divided and vulnerable. They could attack the welfare state in principle and risk losing the votes of many of its beneficiaries (this happened on the Social Security issue). Also, such an attack, in light of the known interests of many New Deal opponents, could easily and correctly be identified with a callous lack of concern and a selfish desire to hold on to existing privileges. Roosevelt was wonderfully blessed by his enemies. The only other alternative for the Republicans was a "me too" approach, with telling criticism only of New Deal contradictions, political trickery, or administrative sloppiness. But concession in principle would have alienated many of the Republican supporters.

Roosevelt's campaign, as usual, was effective. Combined with the weakness of Alfred Landon and his poorly managed effort, it certainly helped raise a sure victory to a landslide. Like the "bloody shirt" of old, the "Hoover depression" continued to form the backdrop, as it would for twenty years. Roosevelt exploited the past darkness and by his warm vibrancy heightened the present light. The New Deal had saved the country, but its work was incomplete. Unlike 1932, he identified the devils— the economic royalists who ran the country until 1932, who had abdicated briefly, who now tried to block every effective reform, and who were trying to come back to power through a Republican victory. But he carefully discriminated between ethical men of wealth and monopolists, trying at least to retain small business support. He emphasized his desire to preserve our basic institutions and took credit for saving free enterprise. But it was a much more aggressive, even provocative campaign than in 1932, with angry jabs at economic autocracy, organized money, economic tyranny, and forces of selfishness and of lust for power. He appealed directly to the poor as he berated the rich and won heavy support from the old Republican progressives, from labor, from former socialists, and from farmers everywhere.

Roosevelt's 1936 campaign could be compared only with that of Jackson in 1832. It even lacked the specificity of Bryan's in 1896, since he announced no dramatic new policies or programs. It was a highly personal appeal, in which he asked voter approval primarily for himself. He would master the sinister forces of evil. He played on old fears, capitalized on immediate gratitude, exploited future hopes. Vast audiences gathered to pay homage and express their love. Never before, at least since Washington, had a candidate so captured the affection of a large majority of the American people, even as his very political success embittered an opposing minority.

In the thirties, as in critical periods of the past, the cult of personality characterized politics everywhere. It was a decade of strong men. Issues were confused or beyond comprehension. No clear public philosophy either explained the depression or clarified policies sufficient to overcome it, just as the terrible abyss of war at the end of the decade was beyond comprehension. People seemed to lack courage, to relinquish freedom, to surrender to their leaders. In Europe both Stalin and Hitler, abetted by a vast apparatus of propaganda and coercion, built regimes as much around personality as around ideology. After the fumbling thirties, only the eloquence, the tenacious courage, the conventional beliefs of a wartime Churchill could rally a confused England. In America, Roosevelt, unable to clarify the complexity of events even for himself, yet stood above events, a knight in shining armor, master of his own fate and invincible. With him we could all win the victory. Confused and inarticulate millions, flooded with feelings but often unable to focus them on issues, poured them out upon a man and upon a symbol—a symbol of hope, victory, concern, good will.

The depression decade invited vast, often guided expressions of mass approval. The election of 1936 came as close to a plebiscite as any other in American history. Roosevelt was clearly the issue. With more success than any preceding politician, save possibly Jackson, he convinced most of those who voted for him that he was for the people (whatever the term "people" really means). His programs were their programs; his enemies their enemies. In fact, opposition to Roosevelt was automatically opposition to the people by a selfish minority. Of course, Roosevelt was a little like the advertiser who proudly displays a product as one needed and long demanded by the public, even as he creates the demand and without his ever having to discuss the merit of the product. They wanted a New Deal. With their help he gave it to them, and would extend it even further if they would join him in mastering their common enemies. At this level, the contradictions of policy, the lack of a future blueprint, the futility of many programs, the failure of others, and the continuation of vast unemployment all became irrelevant and meaningless. Roosevelt could conquer these minor difficulties, just as he conquered polio, Hoover, and the old order, and beat down the grasping plutocrats. With him at the helm, the future would take care of itself.

It is easy to label the Roosevelt of 1936 a demagogue, but at the same time rather pointless. His appeal was emotional and should have been. Partisan politics is not a type of disinterested, dispassionate inquiry. Certainly, with less success, a desperate Landon resorted to even worse diatribes than Roosevelt. American elections too often had contained little else. But Hoover, in 1932, with plenty of passion, had also discussed serious and fundamental issues. In 1912 Wilson made his campaign into a course in political theory. Even in 1936 Roosevelt gave several speeches devoted in a general way to New Deal programs and the country's needs. But since even his speech writers represented diverse points of view, neither in the campaign nor in

1937 was he able to chart a new path. Often he was lost in indecision, as if groping for some new path of action. Roosevelt still had not reached definite conclusions about economic policy. He never quite chose between coordinated planning and decentralization. In 1936, two agricultural programs existed side by side—the AAA and RA—one trying to limit production within the existing system, the other trying to increase it while reforming the system. About the only clear focus was welfare, whatever the contradictions of individual programs, and closely connected the old political appeal to the common man. Roosevelt was thus ill-equipped in 1936 for other than a personal appeal for support or a very broad class appeal.

Even the class appeal had to be vague. The plain man was a constant theme for Roosevelt. He often dramatized and personalized his programs by reference to a farmer or a taxi driver. His speeches emphasized the small people, the average, simple, honest people. Thus he formed a bond of sympathy and slowly bettered the image of the federal government for millions. But Roosevelt was not the simple man that he seemed. Neither was he a farmer, although he often so labeled himself. Nor did he narrow his appeal to just the poor. He had tolerance even for the honest millionaire. What he really wanted was a near classless conglomerate of disparate people, all supporting him. Only large business enterprise was clearly excluded until it proved its loyalty. Such a broad consensus cannot exist except at the level of personality and very general policy, or at the level of ideology. In crisis or in war it can be created around such basic themes as nationalism or the desire for survival. One tack for a politician is to manufacture, or at least overemphasize, emergencies. In 1932 Roosevelt had an authentic, exploitable emergency, and he surely made the best of it. But only the echo of such an emergency remained in 1936. He did not create a new one, although his opponents believed he moved too far in that direction. He did not picture his enemies as overwhelming dangers to the country, threatening its very survival. Had he done so, the label demagogue would have been correct. Instead of such a crisis mentality, he relied upon personal appeal. He succeeded because of the lack of effective opposition, the appeal of various New Deal programs, his persuasive talents, and a general willingness to trust in his leadership. His victory left a shattered but reparable Republican party. More important, it almost destroyed the political left in American politics, whether the dogmatic fringe groups or the terribly honest American Socialist party. As a result, many responsible critics of the New Deal would now speak from a vacuum of power, and were rarely heard, let alone heeded. This was a loss, and one compounded when war and then cold war made radical criticism a type of heresy.

The temporary dominance of one party, particularly in the new Congress, invited intraparty factionalism. Roosevelt had failed to build a new Democratic party around his New Deal programs or to lessen the divergence of belief and interests within that party. In his first term, Roosevelt had formed alliances with Democratic leaders representing all shades of opinion. He had scrupulously avoided direct interference in state primaries and, with only a few exceptions, had lent personal support to even those Southern Democrats who were openly horrified at most New Deal legislation. Yet in the legislative battles of 1935 he had exhausted most of his political capital even with moderate Democrats. Often he ignored young Democratic congressmen who were safely loyal to New Deal programs. By 1937 he had neither won acceptance of a clear program nor even begun to refashion his party around such a program. By then it was much too late to begin.

The very techniques that made the New Deal a political success in 1936 made it vulnerable in 1937. The cult of personality, which bypasses debate, can be as treacherous as unswerving dogmatism, which refuses to engage in essential debate. Roosevelt persuaded people to accept, even want, certain individual programs, but he rarely reeducated them politically. He mediated between divergent advisers but never found a firm path of his own or calculated strategy in terms of unified, long-range goals. He built a new political coalition, but one held together by the glue of personality and by promises to everyone. Many New Deal programs, necessitated by events or pushed by able men, were not only enduring but carefully conceived. The adventitious successes of the New Deal may have been close to the possible. But no core of political principles, no clear economic philosophy, no new clarification of the dilemmas of constitutional democracy resulted. Thus the cult of personality too easily became the meandering of personal whim. Only trial and error remained, hopefully rescued from disaster by good will. If, at some political risk, Roosevelt had been a more disciplined and, in the best sense of the word, dogmatic, person, had worked out a political philosophy and firm policies during his first term, and then had asked for a mandate in their behalf in 1936, he would at least have insured a better informed electorate. He would also have alienated some devotees, invited more effective opposition, made possible a real debate, and possibly prepared the way for a Democratic defeat in 1938 or even 1940.

Between the mindless inflexibility of his less astute critics and Roosevelt's highly personal and unfocused leadership, there is always—remote, difficult, frustrating—the possibility of a true experimentalism, which was as foreign to Roosevelt as it is to the American political tradition. It is the advocacy, in terms of what is known, of tentative solutions, as comprehensive, as systematic, as consistent, as formally perfect as possible, and then as careful a testing of the tentative answer as circumstances permit (at the political level they often permit very little). For example, in 1936 Roosevelt, if he had wanted to remain consistent with his support of our most entrenched institutions, and had understood the implications of this support, could have campaigned as a new disciple of Keynes and of his indirect techniques for attaining recovery and growth. This would have made clear his commitment to a slightly modified corporate capitalism. Such a stand would have challenged the people's understanding and given the opposition a clear target. If he had won, he could have claimed an unambiguous mandate. If he had lost, other alternatives might have been tried, such as a more business-oriented and economically orthodox Republicanism, or

Tugwell's structural planning, or a socialist type of government ownership, or, most radical of all, a sincere effort to restore property and individual enterprise. Without a clear mandate, the glorious victory of 1936 left Roosevelt helpless in dealing with Congress, particularly when many Democrats turned against his personal rule, against his advisers, and against New Deal programs. Then he suffered from the angels, and there was no recourse and no further New Deal.

Through 1935 the New Deal was very much a personalized endeavor. The swing to executive initiative even in legislation stretched back to Wilson and beyond. It climaxed in Roosevelt. But, contrary to conventional views, Congress did not abdicate in the thirties. It was willing and receptive, not prostrate. In the first New Deal Congress, Roosevelt often moderated the restless radicalism of anxious legislators. In 1935, the initiative of most welfare legislation came from Congress and not from the administration. What was unprecedented was the delegation of such extensive powers to a peacetime president. The NIRA, the Thomas Amendment, and the Emergency Relief Appropriation of 1935 were extreme examples. As in war, executive orders replaced detailed congressional acts.

The personal dimension was also evident in the interplay of cabinet and agency heads. They often defended their programs before congressional committees, but even more they tried to gain access to Roosevelt (the "Boss") and capture his support. If there is any consistency in the vast array of diaries and memoirs by the New Deal family, it is in a common testimony to Roosevelt's tremendous ability to keep a diverse, often jealous and petty group of people working as a team. He was a good captain. By planted gossip, a wink, a note of congratulation, a contagious burst of appreciative laughter, a very private joke, a shared secret, he kept even angry competitors happy. Everyone felt at the very center of things, and especially close to Roosevelt. In this sense Roosevelt was a superb administrator. But the very system invited a very loose, haphazard, day-to-day process of decision making, with abrupt shifts of policy. As an arbitrary chief, Roosevelt worked his way through contending forces and reached his own decisions. Often he seemed to betray loyal supporters or to reverse himself on clear commitments. Yet he demanded complete loyalty from his staff, whatever the extent of internal jealousy or disagreement. He quickly and without mercy booted those who would not give this loyalty. On the other hand, he hated to hurt even the incompetents who loved and trusted him and who followed every twist in administration policy. He discharged them reluctantly and, if possible, deviously in order to avoid the pain.

To call Roosevelt a dictator is as meaningless as calling him a demagogue. A powerful office in any case, the early presidency under Roosevelt was a near dictatorial office. He could make many vital decisions on his own, and did. Many of his decisions were inscrutable, highly personal, and thus quite arbitrary. He did what he wanted, and often seemed a man of whim. He disliked set procedures or rules. He was almost as unbureaucratic and as unpredictable as possible. But he very much wanted to act in the public interest. He loved the people and never questioned the election process but instead put tremendous stress upon it. His fireside reports, his wonderfully pleasant news conferences, his love of campaigning, his responsiveness to an audience all made him a representative leader. He even shared many of the illusions of the masses and with sincerity appealed to them. If he failed to raise the level of political discourse, it was from personal inadequacy and not from a desire to deceive. He persuaded himself more easily than others.

In 1936 Roosevelt clearly had the support of a large majority of the people. When they voted for him, they presumably also voted for the New Deal and its continuation. Sixty percent approved, whatever their degree of understanding. They confirmed Roosevelt's own sense of righteousness and confirmed his distaste for his more vocal critics. Yet already the courts had nullified much New Deal legislation. And by 1935 Congress was becoming restless and increasingly concerned about the power it had surrendered in a time of crisis. Key sections of the NIRA and the Agricultural Adjustment Act fell before the courts, while a Congress susceptible to lobbying influences had dwarfed a major tax bill and, on a test vote forced by Roosevelt, had weakened the utilities bill. Roosevelt detested such flagrant defiance of the majority's will and of his own will. A man who usually had his way, and now seemed worthy of it by democratic choice and moral right, fought back. As a democrat, he refused to acquiesce in the institutional barriers that often nullified the will of the majority or even to fight back by means legitimized by these same institutions.

The United States claims to be both a democracy, in which the will of the people is supreme, and a constitutional republic, or a government of law, in which established principles prevail over the whim of a majority or the assertions of a popular leader. Abstractly conceived, the conflict between the two is complete. In American practice the conflict has usually been muted. Not in the New Deal. Roosevelt, burdened to carry out the will of the people, angered at threats to his own power and good intentions, tried to remove the impediment of law. By suggesting that Congress give him, in effect, the power to bring the Supreme Court into line with administrative policies, he moved toward a more complete democracy, or a government more directly responsive to the will of the majority. In a decade of propaganda, of highly emotional and irrational political movements, of charismatic leaders, this proposed shift in government aroused opposition from all sides and most fervently from civil libertarians.

The Court Bill of 1937 was ostensibly a reform measure. In fact, it was a perfectly transparent instrument for permitting Roosevelt to make enough extra, pro-New Deal appointments to the Supreme Court to alter the close decisions on New Deal legislation. The device was a provision allowing extra appointments for unretired judges over the age of seventy. Roosevelt plotted the bill in secrecy, sprung it by complete surprise on Congress, defended it by hypocritical arguments, and then pushed it by every political trick, every type of ruthless pressure and cunning he possessed. The central issue was not the constitutionality of New Deal measures, or the incapacity of the existing Court. It had been quite vigorous in its frequent dissent but also continuously divided. At issue was an institutional arrangement, in part rooted in the Constitution, in part a product of tradition. The Supreme Court early gained the right of constitutional review, or the power to nullify acts of Congress on appeal of aggrieved litigants. It could do this when, in its judgment, such acts violated the terms of the Constitution, the highest and most stable expression of popular will.

Just as much as Roosevelt, the Supreme Court judges represented power, not drawn as directly from the people but nonetheless anchored in the public acceptance of constitutionalism and of appointed, life-tenured judges to interpret the Constitution. The Court issue also gave the concealed opponents of Roosevelt a made-to-order opportunity to switch sides or vent previously unvoiced grievances. Thus the Court battle was a struggle in power politics as well as in grand principles of government. The Court won and Roosevelt lost. But only after a long, agonizing congressional session, during which one judge retired and the switch of one vote in a crucial decision (often falsely viewed as a political move by the Court) changed the whole obstructionist profile of the Court and initiated a permanent change toward broader economic regulation.

Just as Roosevelt found the limits of his power in the Court fight, so the Supreme Court probed its limits in the thirties. The Supreme Court, as the president, had a limited amount of power. Back of both, back of a balanced system of government, were the beliefs and habits of a people. Law, particularly constitutional law, exists as a stabilizing, restraining influence on popular government, equally preserving entrenched privilege and preventing new tyranny, particularly that dressed in the popular fashion of the mob. But Court restraints cannot permanently impede something desired by a vast majority. Fortunately, the amendment process provides a technique, although a difficult technique, for achieving change, as does the more informal process of changing interpretation. Roosevelt wanted a quicker answer and believed he had enough support to secure it. By implication, he wanted to politicize the Court so as to secure a constitution that could, like the English, be amended by legislative action instead of the more cumbersome American practice of having the people act in a special constitutional capacity. He also wanted to restrict the nonelective legislative power disguised in the right of constitutional review. Felix Frankfurter, a major adviser and in the tradition of Oliver W. Holmes, also believed that the courts should not lightly challenge legislative will, and never if they could find any interpretative leeway.

The sharply divided Supreme Court of the thirties did not represent clear juristic theories. As yet, no historian has seriously studied the Court fight. Much the pity, for here was probably the most important issue to arise in the New Deal. The important cases show no clear pattern, except a near unanimity of opposition to expansion of federal power by four judges, a willingness to support most Roosevelt policies by three judges, and a general willingness by all judges to wade boldly into the constitutional issues raised by the legislative flood. Like the Warren Court later, the judges rejected a narrow doctrine of judicial restraint. Or, like Roosevelt, they did not hesitate to use the power they possessed. They overturned New Deal legislation for several reasons—undue delegation of legislative power, overextension of the commerce clause, denial of due process and of contract rights, and, in one important state case on minimum wages, because of a balancing of technical issues rather than a substantive issue. The Court was most atavistic in its narrow interpretation of interstate commerce and thus in limiting the range of federal economic regulation; most prophetic in censoring new administrative procedures on libertarian grounds, and, often led by the so-called conservative foursome in unheralded cases, in strictly upholding the rights of free speech and press.

The Court fight wasted a congressional session, helped destroy the Roosevelt myth of invincibility, disillusioned many of his former disciples, divided the Democratic party, gave the Republican party a new lease on life, and left Roosevelt bitter and hurt. As always, he became deeply involved in the battle and scarcely remembered what was at issue. In his frustration he exhibited his worst and most militant character traits and thus further aided his opponents. But there was partial redemption for Roosevelt. Some of his most bitter enemies came out even worse. Their onslaught of cheap propaganda, including shabby tricks, outright lies, and fantastic charges, made Roosevelt look like a gentleman.

The Court fight was followed by a new depression, by an increasingly hostile Congress, and by few significant legislative achievements. In the wake of this, Roosevelt renewed his battle for popular democracy. As a consistent postlude to the Supreme Court battle, he used the campaign of 1938 to attempt a minor but controversial rationalization of his own political party. Later, in an overture to Wendell Willkie, he would try to get a new party system, with what he called a progressive, conservative realignment. In the Court fight Roosevelt lost control of congressional Democrats. Just as effectively as the courts, large numbers dared oppose him and, as he saw it, the people who elected him. Roosevelt felt that a national mandate, won by a single party leader and on a party platform, should bind the party in Congress, both to himself and to the platform (he easily blurred the two). Thus he wanted to be prime minister and control a loyal legislative majority. He correctly believed this necessary for responsive democracy. In this case he battled not the written Constitution, with its strict separation of powers, but an unwritten one—the vast, entrenched apparatus of broad-interest, nonideological political parties, rooted in thousands of local machines, local power structures, and local economic interests. This loose, undisciplined party system, except in crisis, made complete party discipline impossible and invited all manner of shifting coalitions, often against the president and against popular desires.

As the Supreme Court, the loose party system served many holy and unholy purposes. It often allowed minority regional interests to frustrate national purpose, provided a cloak for divisive and selfish economic interests, and often stymied the legislative process, but it also represented a lever to resist presidential foolishness, a solvent for political extremists, and a brake on crisis-inspired haste. Just as so-called liberals joined Frankfurter to denounce activists and absolutists on the New Deal Court, only later to join the activist and absolutist Warren Court in its battle against majority-supported security legislation and "witch-hunting," so the same "liberals" who chafed at legislative impediments to Roosevelt or his New Deal applauded Congress later when it offered some slight resistance to Lyndon Johnson's foreign policy or when Congress used the Watergate scandals to wrench power away from a president they did not respect. But Roosevelt, as an often frustrated president, was most aware of party obstructionism. He asked a few states to reject Democratic "conservatives" in their 1938 primaries and threatened a half-dozen sacred cows of American politics. The results for Roosevelt were disastrous, with only one possible victory for all his efforts and a world of resentment to face in the new Congress. Yet these battle scars did not destroy the personal appeal of Roosevelt as candidate. He could still win the people much more consistently than their representatives. Again, this illustrated his failure to win an informed acceptance of ideas and policies.

Beginning in August of 1937, the most precipitous economic decline in American history added a new burden to Roosevelt's vale of tears. Brief but dramatic, the depression leveled out in mid-1938. But it hurt while it lasted. Hopeful workers, finally reemployed in 1935 or 1936, faced new and lengthy layoffs. Unemployment, so difficult to ascertain in the thirties, probably dropped to a temporary low of from six to seven million in early 1937, only to soar to about eleven million by 1938. Other indexes are quite clear. The stock market fell by 43 percent. Industrial production, which reached the 1929 level by October, 1936, and slowly climbed beyond it, declined by one-third, or over halfway back to the lowest level of 1933. Quarterly profits, which had never reached the 1929 level, fell by 82 percent. Income had risen to within 12 percent of 1929, only to drop by over 12 percent, almost exactly paralleled by wholesale prices. While wages held firm, payrolls declined by 35 percent, indicating the degree of unemployment or part-time work. In all, the economy plunged about one-half as much in nine months as it had from 1929 to 1933, and with attendant human costs. A lag in resuming relief created almost as much dire suffering as in 1932. Yet the decline was not as shocking as in the early thirties. A nation inured to depression half expected another. Even the semblance of a boom in early 1937 had created fears. A cycle complex was deeply embedded. Those laid off were resigned rather than bitter.

The depression intensified the political passions of the decade. In just retribution, Republicans almost gleefully referred to the "Roosevelt depression." Almost without exception, the business community blamed the depression on New Deal policies—on threatening taxes, the coddling of organized labor, budgetary deficits, a political philosophy contrary to accepted economic procedures, and such attacks on free enterprise and on business leaders as to discourage private investment. The depression was the inevitable result of a government conspiracy to overthrow capitalism. In indignation, Roosevelt retorted with equal passion and irrelevance. In his terms, business was the culprit. He lambasted the old bugaboo of a government-induced lack of confidence, and vaguely talked of a deliberate business conspiracy against the New Deal, a callous strike of capital to embarrass him and frustrate his reform efforts. After underplaying the severity of the depression, New Deal officials settled on the official doctrine that the "recession" resulted from monopoly and from artificially high prices that undercut consumption. This explanation abetted the trust busting of Thurman Arnold and influenced the voluminous investigation of economic concentration carried out by a Temporary National Economic Committee. But behind the emotional bombast and public posturing, a confused Roosevelt carried on discussions with business leaders and considered a new NRA.

There can be no exact ranking of the many causes of the 1937 depression. The vaunted but uneven recovery of 1936 was fragile. Unemployment remained high. Construction was still in deep depression. Short-term investments prevailed over long-term. In late 1936 a boomlet, tied to veterans' bonuses (granted in spite of Roosevelt's opposition), relief expenditures, and a surge of industrial orders, led to price increases and inflation-hedging advance purchasing, which set the stage for a decline unless a more rapid tempo of growth could be maintained throughout 1937. Governmental policies, instead of supporting such growth, actually inhibited it. The beginning collection of Social Security taxes cut down on wages. A drastic curtailment of relief expenditures in 1937, plus the termination of the PWA, further reduced purchasing power. For the first time in years, the government cash budget was in balance. Also, in two moves in response to banking and business fears of inflation, the Federal Reserve Board, without rejecting an easy-money policy, nonetheless raised the reserve requirements of member banks. Although idle funds usually covered the rise without direct economic effects, the move did lead to some local increases in interest rates and had an inhibitory effect on a depression-jittery society. Thus the whole burden of sustained growth passed to private business, which tossed it right back in the form of an embarrassing depression.

In the private sector, both investors and executives were excessively sensitive to minute changes in profits and profit expectations. Profits, so low in the early thirties, leveled off in early 1937, still below the 1929 level. Pressed by higher wage levels and aggressive unions, bled of large cash reserves by a hasty distribution of dividends in 1936 to beat the new, undistributed profits tax, angry at government inaction during the wave of sit-down strikes in 1936, facing rising prices for raw materials, and still overreacting to misinterpreted New Deal policies, corporate leaders simply refused to make enough long-term commitments to maintain high employment and a growing national product.

The depression proved that the New Deal had not yet mastered economic cycles. It also showed how little the basic economic structure had been altered by four years of legislative change. Private individuals or private groups still made the major economic decisions. They could or could not invest as they pleased, spend or not spend, produce more or less, raise or lower prices, be happy with profits of 5 percent or wait out a major debacle in hopes of 6 percent. This being true, the emotional warfare between government and business was a further disaster, making recovery even more difficult. The New Deal had provided welfare safeguards for some individuals, who now "luxuriated" with their first unemployment checks. At best, these had only a small impact on the economy. The government still had the same unused alternatives: to force the amount and kind of investment it wanted by tax policy and rigid controls, or to bail out the flagging private economy by creating a profitable market through vast spending efforts.

Everyone had a proffered cure for the depression. Business leaders wanted a pat on the shoulder, tax relief, and a balanced national budget. The pat was politically impossible; the tax cut would have helped stimulate recovery, but its benefits could have been lost by the cuts in government spending necessitated by a balanced budget. Yet, as usual, the businessmen made as much economic sense as politicians. The most influential New Deal advisers, such as Corcoran or a dedicated, increasingly favored Hopkins, wanted deficit spending (roughly similar in effect to a tax cut) and monopoly busting, which, if seriously attempted, would have so disrupted business activity as to nullify any effect from limited welfare spending. No one proposed a medicine directed at more than the symptoms.

The medicine actually used was pure Keynes. Very quickly it relieved the pain. The patient was soon as well as it had ever been in the thirties—but only after Roosevelt floundered for months in greater indecision than had Hoover in 1930 and 1931. Finally, in April, 1938, without any real conversion to Keynesian doctrine, he decided to spend. In a near duplicate of 1935, a huge deficit appropriation reinvigorated the WPA, restored the PWA, and gave needed zest to the FSA. Almost everyone agrees that this was the major factor in sparking a revival. The antimonopoly action did not aid recovery. It was half political window dressing, half an enormous fact-finding enterprise. Business won some honor points on its plan. Increasing minorities in Congress were applying the shoulder pat. Congress repealed the undistributed profits tax and reduced capital gains taxes. The spending and tax relief were reinforcing remedies, almost equally relevant to an upturn but politically at opposite poles.

Even as the revival began, European economies were already responding to larger defense budgets. By 1940, our own military preparations began to replace social welfare, and eventually far outstripped it, as the main type of government investment. Military priorities became ever more an overt and permanent subsidy to the managerial elite of America, with others who could manage it picking up the delicious crumbs created by growth or guaranteed by a generous government.

In addition to a reenactment of relief, Roosevelt in 1938 prodded his last New Deal legislation through a reluctant Congress. Picking up the pieces of past programs, Congress gave the farmers a new, giant, noneconomy package. The second Agricultural Adjustment Act provided price supports and continued conservation payments, conditioned on the acceptance of acreage or marketing controls for crops with a surplus. By referendum, all the farmers growing a major staple crop could vote for or against controls. By this, and a restored local committee system, the grass-roots approach continued. Surpluses soon necessitated export sales at government loss or else vast storage expenses. Some surpluses could be justified by Henry Wallace's ever normal granary, based on Joseph's experiences in Egypt. Before there was a glutted market, World War II came to the rescue. The second Agricultural Adjustment Act permanently established the main features of New Deal agricultural policy and added a new crop insurance program. In this sense, and also because it led to bountiful and inexpensive foods and fibers, the policy was a success. But even as support prices brought the efficient farmer parity prices (or 110 percent of parity during the war), small, inefficient farm owners, tenant farmers, and farm laborers suffered. They did not share in most welfare and labor legislation. As a result of improved technology, they slowly became part of the largest agriculture surplus—

a human surplus. The FSA, their own special agency, struggled unsuccessfully against its heretical reputation and, over Roosevelt's ineffectual protest, was eliminated by a wartime Congress. The final major New Deal measure, the Fair Labor Standards Act of 1938, consolidated some of the early gains of the NRA and completed the welfare state. The NRA codes forbade child labor and often set minimum wages and maximum hours. The new bill aimed at these same goals on a permanent basis. The political battle invited strange bedfellows. In effect, northern urban politicians, humane reformers, and large, mature corporations favored the bill. Entrenched labor unions, struggling small businesses, farmers, and the South opposed it. The bill passed in June, 1938, but as usual was trimmed by amendments or limited by the necessity of basing it on the interstate commerce clause. The very laborers who most needed its protection—local extraction, agricultural, domestic, small retail—were excluded. The largest beneficiaries under the original, gradually applied (up to seven years) standards of forty cents and forty hours were southern factory workers. Congress shelved other far-reaching legislation, such as seven proposed new TVAs. The only additional, significant, prewar measure was a reorganization bill in 1939 that allowed Roosevelt to establish the Executive Office of the president, bringing several advisory groups and agencies into a White House staff. This followed a much more revolutionary reorganization bill rejected by Congress in 1938. In 1939 the House rejected even mild housing and spending measures. The New Deal, which began in a burst of energy, simply petered out in 1938 and 1939.

In 1933 Roosevelt exploited a crisis and successfully used his own personal magic on a broad spectrum of politicians. After 1936 he had no such useful crisis. His persuasive powers were insufficient to blur and mute the divergence of interests among congressmen of his own party. In the wake of seeming Republican failures, Roosevelt won a mandate for rapid innovation in 1933. But the new economic crisis of 1937, following hard on his own best efforts, created a psychology of retreat rather than one of advance. It seemed that many Democratic stalwarts returned home again—to state rights, fiscal integrity, and private enterprise. In reality, they had never gone anywhere. They too had abdicated in 1933, but never quite expected to reap such a bitter harvest. Senator Harry Byrd of Virginia perfectly symbolized their unfulfilled hopes, their dilemma, and their defection. He voted for a Cleveland in 1932 but soon found to his dismay that he had helped elect a combination of Theodore Roosevelt, William Jennings Bryan, and Eugene Debs, and with this political hybrid a bullpen of suspicious and heretical intellectuals. Like Raymond Moley, traditional Democratic congressmen could only point back in perplexity to the early Roosevelt— he *had* sounded like Cleveland. The net effect of their disenchantment was an effective opposition coalition in Congress and a stymied president. In domestic politics there was no leverage for significant change. New events would have to create such a leverage.

In 1938, the year of Munich, there also seemed no leeway for major initiatives in foreign policy. But events and presidential persuasion helped create the opportunity. Roosevelt emerged as an internationalist and as an extreme activist in foreign policy. But he had not gone anywhere either. The early New Deal repudiation of Europe was not, for Roosevelt, a repudiation of American power used in behalf of international goals. At most, it was a strategic retreat from a confused Europe in order to consolidate that power. By 1938 the European situation was quite clear to Roosevelt. With his moral horror of fascism, his zest for a worthy fight, and his determination to use all power in his possession for the right, he slowly built the political coalition, in Congress and out, for unencumbered American action. As events dictated, the action was to be as bold, as uncoerced by precedent or even traditional legality as in 1933. Once again he won his way. He was blessed by his enemies, by righteous fervor, by his sense of destiny. He gave America a second transfusion of courage. But as in his futile quest for recovery, he never quite understood the complexity of the problems faced and never provided the essential education for dealing with a postwar world. In 1945 he saw a second glorious victory, a second great vindication, in all ways equal to 1936. But it too was only the false morning glow of a second long day of tears. Death spared him the clear light of that disillusioning day.

The New Deal stopped growing. It did not disappear. A subsidized, regulated welfare capitalism still stands, forty years later, as the core of American domestic policy. The United States has neither moved beyond it nor tried other alternatives, despite the varied and often confused protest movements of the sixties. At best, subsequent presidents have patched a few holes, repaired a few loose shingles, and added some new rooms to the welfare state. Thus the changes of the thirties were not only numerous but prophetic, setting the themes for subsequent political discourse. The welfare measures—social security, labor protection, housing—have all been expanded. None has been repudiated. Both conservation and advisory types of planning have remained as generally accepted ideals, however compromised in practice. Whatever the internal inequities, agriculture, our greatest economic success story, still functions under a subsidized price system and, when needed, production controls. Large business enterprise has learned to accept, if not to love, the protective and only mildly restrictive role of government in maintaining growth and high profits. Likewise, organized labor has shrugged off its earlier militancy and, like a happy but protected lamb, finally lain down beside the business lion.

The same continuity is evident at the political level. Whatever the limitations of Roosevelt, America's political parties have not discovered or created another political leader who could tear away, with the wisdom or the foolishness of a child, so many traditional articles of faith, and thus open up so many pregnant possibilities. Instead, many of his successors have turned fragile New Deal policies into new, binding articles of faith. None has been able to step into the inviting flux, the confused and discordant flux of New Deal policies, and provide what Roosevelt so often lacked—a mature comprehension of complexity, a scholar's ability to make clear and careful distinctions, and a teacher's ability to lift the level of popular understanding.

Within the one inescapable context of the thirties—the need for economic growth—the New Deal was a short-run failure, but it did initiate changes that led to long-run success. It began the final maturation of our economic system, and at least pointed toward the political economy most capable of maximizing production, consumption, profits, and jobs. We are as yet only beginning to exploit the full potential of government credit, incentives, and subsidies, even as we glimpse the sometimes disturbing promise of advertising, automation, and more careful political indoctrination, and even as we finally begin to appreciate some of the unanticipated social costs of unending economic growth.

To emphasize the eventual economic results of New Deal policies is not to evaluate the New Deal as a whole. Almost no one in the New Deal, almost no one in the thirties, even dared predict such long-term economic gains. But, superb irony, few New Dealers expected quite so little in other areas. The fervent New Deal bureaucrats dreamed of a much greater level of social justice, of a truer community, than the United States has as yet achieved. They, of course, wanted more production and more jobs, but they also wanted everyone to have a sense of meaningful involvement and worth. They wanted everyone to be able to consume more, but desired consumption not as a balm for meaninglessness but as a necessary adjunct of a sense of real achievement and fulfillment. They wanted industrial growth and even restored profits, not as ends but as corollaries of widespread opportunities for creative and socially beneficial enterprise.

As these more idealistic New Dealers grew older, they often became tragic figures, seemingly out of touch with things. They looked back in nostalgia to what they had dreamed, and what they had all shared, and what they had longed for. The prosperous but callous fifties seemed a mockery. They talked of how Roosevelt, had he lived, would at last have led them into the kingdom. Like lonely and unneeded soldiers, they cried aloud for their old commander and for the old crusade. If anything seemed clear to them, it was that their dreams and hopes had been betrayed. Instead of responding to the greater efficiency, the accelerating growth, even the new welfare measures of the sixties, they looked on sadly, as if the substance, the moral heart, had been removed from things.

For some of the most perceptive social critics of the thirties, for an Edmund Wilson or a John Dewey, the New Deal was not a promise betrayed; it was essentially misdirected from the beginning. It began and ended with conventional or oversimplified half-answers, answers which the more alienated, more sensitive, and more analytic intellectuals all too easily repudiated. But the more radical critics, despite the early hopes of someone like Tugwell, had no pathway to power. In fact, they can never attain power in a democracy unless conditions produce a passive resignation on the part of citizens, a willingness to relinquish responsibility to angry but largely incomprehensible prophets. In a working democracy the penetrating critic, like a lonely Jeremiah, must teach and often suffer. He cannot dictate. Neither can he win elections. His ringing voice must be heard from the lectern and pulpit. He will never master the soothing art of the fireside—and should not. He is too honest and too clearheaded.

For the historian, every judgment and every evaluation of the past has to be tinged with a pinch of compassion, a sense of the beauty and nobility present even in the frustration of honest hopes and humane ideals. He sees that, from almost any valuative perspective, the thirties could have brought so much more, but also so much worse, than the New Deal. No diverse political movement, responding to multiple pressures, can come close to matching the expectations of any sensitive social critic. The limiting political context has to be understood—the safeguards and impediments of our political system, Roosevelt's intellectual limitations, and most of all the economic ignorance and philosophic immaturity of the American electorate. The plausible alternatives to the New Deal are not easily suggested, particularly if one considers all the confining and limiting circumstances.

From almost any perspective, the New Deal solved a few problems, ameliorated others, obscured many, and created unanticipated new ones. This is about all our political system can generate, even in crisis. If the people knew better and chose better, if they shared similar goals, there would be few crises anyway. If they must know better to have better, then our conventional politics is no answer, except as a perennial interim accommodation with incompatible goals and with ignorance. Even this permits more thorough criticism its long day of persuasion and education.

Only with trepidation will the student of history try to judge the results of the New Deal. He will not do it with a sense of heartless criticism. Not only would it be unfair, but too much is involved. But judge he must, not to whip the past but to use it. For so much that originated or at least matured in the policies of the Roosevelt administration lives on in our present institutions. Thus his rightful criticism is directed at himself, his country, his institutions, his age. If so directed, his evaluation must be just, thorough, and honest; otherwise, he practices only self-deceit.

A Note on New Deal Historiography

The first bountiful harvest of New Deal scholarship is now in hand. We have monographs, of varied quality, on almost every conceivable aspect of the Roosevelt administration. With time, and perspective, the partisan and overtly valuative emphases that so enlivened, or so distorted, the earliest scholarship have all but abated. Mature scholars have also moved beyond such simplistic and puerile questions as, Did the New Deal initiate revolutionary changes? and beyond such ambiguous labels as radical, liberal, or conservative. Increasingly, historians ask precise and very concrete questions: Who supported Roosevelt and why? What economic and social realities lay behind Roosevelt's political success? What groups gained what returns from New Deal policies? What were the enduring consequences of New Deal economic policy? How did new federal policies affect state and local governments? Lamentably, the large number of new monographs, the more sophisticated analysis, has not contributed to new or revised accounts of the whole domestic New Deal. Save for textbooks, largely polemical interpretations, or numerous parasitic anthologies, the student seeking an overview of the New Deal still has to turn to quite dated volumes composed in the fifties or early sixties.

Despite numerous biographies, the Roosevelt personality remains elusive and baffling. All existing biographies seem prefatory or inconclusive. The most extensive and thoughtful completed biography is James M. Burns, *Roosevelt: The Lion and the Fox* and *Roosevelt: The Soldier of Freedom* (New York: Harcourt, Brace, 1965 and 1970). Burns chronicles the dramatic impact of Roosevelt, but stresses his inability to form a political coalition committed to a consistent program of reform. From 1952 to 1956, Frank Freidel published a three-volume biography of the prepresidential Roosevelt [*Franklin D. Roosevelt: The Apprenticeship; . . . The Ordeal*; and . . . *The Triumph* (Boston: Little, Brown)]. Meticulous in scholarship, unencumbered by interpretative schemes, and always honest and balanced, these three volumes provide a definitive account of Roosevelt's early successes and failures. After a long interval, Freidel has completed a fourth volume, *Franklin D. Roosevelt: Launching the New Deal* (Boston: Little, Brown, 1973), but it is much more a political history of the early New Deal than a biography of Roosevelt. Moreover, it encompasses less than a year of Roosevelt's life. More topical biographical studies include Daniel Fusfield's *The Economic Thought of Franklin D. Roosevelt and the Origins of the New Deal* (New York: Columbia University Press, 1956), and a scathingly critical, tortured, but often revealing profile by Edgar E. Robinson, *The Roosevelt Leadership, 1933–1945* (Philadelphia: Lippincott, 1955).

Unfortunately, Roosevelt left little in the way of an autobiography; he rarely wrote his own speeches or even composed self-revealing letters. Thus the most intimate revelations all came from his friends or subordinates, such as in

Frances Perkins's adulatory *The Roosevelt I Knew* (New York: The Viking Press, 1946), and, much more caustic, in *The Secret Diary of Harold Ickes*, 3 vols. (New York: Simon and Schuster, 1953–1954). The two most thoughtful associates of Roosevelt were brain trusters Raymond Moley and Rexford G. Tugwell. Both men fell permanently under the sway of the Roosevelt personality, yet both eventually deplored crucial policy shifts in the New Deal, although from quite different perspectives. Both have continued to reflect upon the Roosevelt years—Moley in more critical terms in *After Seven Years* (New York: Harper Brothers, 1939) and *The First New Deal* (New York: Harcourt, Brace, 1966); Tugwell, with more despair than bitterness, in *The Democratic Roosevelt* (Garden City: Doubleday, 1957), *The Brains Trust* (New York: Viking, 1968), and *In Search of Roosevelt* (Cambridge: Harvard University Press, 1972).

Early one-volume histories of the New Deal (by Basil Rauch, Dexter Perkins, and Mario Einaudi) were all superseded in 1963 by William E. Leuchtenburg's *Franklin D. Roosevelt and the New Deal* (New York: Harper & Row). Leuchtenburg encompasses both domestic and foreign policy, and combines careful synthesis with original scholarship. Sympathetic to most New Deal policies, he was still much more critical than most earlier historians. In both scope and calculated literary appeal, the major history of the early New Deal is Arthur Schlesinger, Jr.'s, three-volume *Age of Roosevelt*—I. *The Crisis of the Old Order*; II. *The Coming of the New Deal*; III. *The Politics of Upheaval* (New York: Houghton, Mifflin, 1957–1960), a vast undertaking that remains conspicuously uncontinued after a lapse of fifteen years. Schlesinger is overtly partisan, a fan of Roosevelt and the New Deal, yet accepts scholarly discipline and incorporates abundant factual detail, much of which is now being superseded by more detailed monographs. His forte is sharp even if often unfair characterization, and a fluent even if superficial interpretative scheme which apotheosizes Roosevelt's nontheoretical and opportunistic leadership.

Several more topical books, by New Deal critics as well as admirers, relate to the New Deal as a whole. Among the best of these are Otis Graham's *Encore for Reform: The Old Progressives and the New Deal* (New York: Oxford, 1967); James T. Patterson's *Congressional Conservatism and the New Deal* (Lexington: University of Kentucky Press, 1967) and *The New Deal and the States: Federalism in Transition* (Princeton: Princeton University Press, 1969); and R. Alan Lawson's *The Failure of Independent Liberalism, 1930–1941* (New York: G. P. Putnam's Sons, 1971), a perceptive analysis of non-Marxist critics of the New Deal. The following two critical appraisals of recent American politics relate closely to the enduring consequences of the New Deal: Grant McConnell, *Private Power and American Democracy* (New York: Knopf, 1961), and Theodore Lowi, *The End of Liberalism* (New York: W. W. Norton, 1969).

Beyond these broad studies, the careful student will have to turn to more narrow and usually more descriptive monographs, or to more restricted syntheses or biographies. Even here, a few very critical books are conspicuously unwritten or unpublished: a history of the crucial Court fight of 1937 (the story is obliquely available in journalistic accounts, in histories of the Supreme Court, and in biographies of Supreme Court judges), an integrated history of conservation or of resource management policies, a full account of the total agricultural program, or histories of either the total relief program or new welfare services.

Since all New Deal programs had an economic dimension, the student is now fortunate to have an unusually clear and yet technically sophisticated economic profile in Lester V. Chandler's *America's Greatest Depression, 1929–1941* (New York: Harper & Row, 1970). Several broad economic treatises contain excellent chapters on the New Deal: Milton Friedman and Anna Jacobson Schwartz, *A Monetary History of the United States* (Princeton: Princeton University Press, 1963); Herbert V. Prichnow, ed., *The Federal Reserve System* (New York: Harper, 1960); Randolph E. Paul, *Taxation for Prosperity* (New York: Bobbs-Merrill, 1947); and E. A. Goldenweiser, *American Monetary Policy* (New York: McGraw-Hill, 1950). Marriner Eccles, in large part the architect of New Deal central banking policy, documents his early Keynesian views in *Beckoning Frontiers* (New York: Knopf, 1951). For Keynes's impact, see Robert

Lekachman, *The Age of Keynes* (New York: Random House, 1966).

New Deal agricultural policy was exceedingly complex. It is no surprise that one has to consult numerous monographs to get the full story. In a model monograph, Van L. Perkins explores the first, critical year of the AAA in *Crisis in Agriculture: The Agricultural Adjustment Administration and the New Deal, 1933* (Berkeley: University of California Press, 1969). This adds detail to two earlier policy studies: Gilbert Fite, *George N. Peek and the Fight for Farm Parity* (Norman: University of Oklahoma Press, 1954), and Richard S. Kirkendall, *Social Scientists and Farm Policies in the Age of Roosevelt* (Columbia: University of Missouri Press, 1966). Efforts at farm relief, or internal reform of agriculture, have proved more enticing to historians than mainline recovery efforts. The class-conscious efforts of the RA and FSA are detailed in Sidney Baldwin, *Poverty and Politics: The Rise and Fall of the Farm Security Administration* (Chapel Hill: University of North Carolina Press, 1968), in Bernard Sternsher, *Rexford G. Tugwell and the New Deal* (New Brunswick: Rutgers University Press, 1964), and in Paul K. Conkin, *Tomorrow a New World: The New Deal Community Program* (Ithaca: Cornell University Press, 1958). The most lowly farmers receive their due in David Conrad, *The Forgotten Farmers: The Story of the Sharecroppers in the New Deal* (Urbana: University of Illinois Press, 1965).

Ellis W. Hawley's *The New Deal and the Problem of Monopoly, 1933–39* (Princeton: Princeton University Press, 1965), is not only the best survey of ambivalent New Deal policies toward large business enterprise, but also the most comprehensive account of the NRA. It is balanced by Irwin Bernstein's *The Turbulent Years: A History of the American Worker, 1933–1941* (Boston: Houghton, Mifflin, 1970).

Only detailed monographs chart Roosevelt's resource management initiatives. A broad array of source material is in Edgar B. Nixon, ed., *Franklin D. Roosevelt and Conservation, 1911–1945*, 2 vols. (Washington: Government Printing Office, 1957). For soil conservation, see Marion Clawson and R. Burnell Held, *Soil Conservation in Perspective* (Baltimore: Johns Hopkins

University Press, 1967); for the story of the CCC, John A. Salmond, *The Civilian Conservation Corps, 1933–1942: A New Deal Case Study* (Durham: Duke University Press, 1967). The TVA was a major story in itself, but one not yet well told in its entirety by any historian. Thus a student must consult the following, self-descriptive topical studies: Preston J. Hubbard, *Origins of the TVA: The Muscle Shoals Controversy, 1920–1932* (Nashville: Vanderbilt University Press, 1961); C. Herman Pritchett, *The Tennessee Valley Authority: A Study in Public Administration* (Chapel Hill: University of North Carolina Press, 1943); Philip Selznick, *TVA and the Grass Roots: A Study in the Sociology of Formal Organization* (Berkeley: University of California Press, 1949); William H. Droze, *High Dams and Slack Waters: TVA Rebuilds a River* (Baton Rouge: Louisiana University Press, 1965); Norman I. Wengert, *Valley of Tomorrow: The TVA and Agriculture* (Knoxville: Bureau of Public Administration, University of Tennessee, 1952); and Thomas K. McCraw, *Morgan vs. Lilienthal: The Feud Within the TVA* (Chicago: Loyola University Press, 1970) and *TVA and the Power Fight, 1933–1939* (Philadelphia: Lippincott, 1971).

The broad array of relief and welfare measures has defied any unified treatment. In fact, we do not yet have an adequate history even of the WPA, although we have numerous monographs on the several arts projects. The best overview of relief policies is in Searle F. Charles, *Minister of Relief: Harry Hopkins and the Depression* (Syracuse: Syracuse University Press, 1963). For Social Security, see Roy Lubove, *The Struggle for Social Security, 1900–1935* (Cambridge: Harvard University Press, 1968), and Edwin E. Witte, *The Development of the Social Security Act* (Madison: University of Wisconsin Press, 1962); for housing, see Robert M. Fisher, *Twenty Years of Public Housing* (New York: Harper, 1959), and Timothy McDonnell, S.J., *The Wagner Housing Act: A Case Study of the Legislative Process* (Chicago: Loyola University Press, 1957). For the relationship of the New Deal to minorities, see Raymond Wolters, *Negroes and the Great Depression: The Problem of Economic Recovery* (Westport, Conn.: Greenwood, 1970), and Bernard Sternsher, ed., *The Negro in Depression and War* (Chicago: Quadrangle, 1969).

INDEX